Find Your Path *to* Resilience

Powerful techniques to build emotional strength

I0799528

Quarto

First published in 2025 by Leaping Hare Press,
an imprint of The Quarto Group.
One Triptych Place
London, SE1 9SH,
United Kingdom
T (0)20 7700 9000
www.Quarto.com

EEA Representation, WTS Tax d.o.o., Žanova ulica 3, 4000
Kranj, Slovenia
www.wts-tax.si

A catalogue record for this book is available from the British Library.

ISBN 978-1-8360-0697-8
Ebook ISBN 978-1-8360-0698-5

10 9 8 7 6 5 4 3 2 1

Text designed and typeset by Dinah Drazin
Illustrations on pages 27 and 101 by DKB Creative Ltd

Editorial Director: Monica Perdoni
Commissioning Editor: Sophie Lazar
Editor: Katerina Menhennet
Senior Designer: Renata Latipova
Senior Production Controller: Rohana Yusof

Printed in the UK CPI092025

MIX
Paper | Supporting responsible forestry
FSC® C013604
FSC
www.fsc.org

Find Your Path *to* Resilience

Powerful techniques to build emotional strength

Byron Athene

Leaping Hare Press

Dedication

For my wife, for her consistent support and inspiration.

For my clients, who have helped me shape my ideas with their interpretation and feedback.

Contents

Introduction 7

CHAPTER ONE
Quick Tips to Rebuild Resilience 13

CHAPTER TWO
The Fundamentals of Reality 43

CHAPTER THREE
Reframing 57

CHAPTER FOUR
Emotions 71

CHAPTER FIVE
Splitting the Emotional Atom 85

CHAPTER SIX
The Growth Mindset 99

CHAPTER SEVEN
Reimagining Anxiety 111

CHAPTER EIGHT
Memory Reconsolidation 119

CHAPTER NINE
Reparenting 133

CHAPTER TEN
Where Do We Go From Here? 147

Endnotes 157
Index 158

Introduction

If you ask ten people what the word 'resilience' means to them, you may get ten slightly different responses that revolve around a recurring theme: withstanding challenges and bouncing back from them. Whatever the word means to you, this book will help you naturally inhabit that definition, as well as the dictionary definition. At times, you may find it challenging to be as resilient as you'd like to be because of the situation and/or the mood you're in. But, bearing a few things in mind, it's clear that situations and moods don't matter nearly as much as you think they do. Let's begin.

First a bit of personal history to provide some context.

I have two older brothers, and we all have stutters. My theory is that the oldest brother developed one, the middle brother copied him, and I copied them both. I remember being able to control it at first – switch it on and off – but there was an incident when I was eight where I stuttered in front of my class and the whole class laughed at me. *I'll come back to this shortly.* After that I was no longer able to control the fluency of my speech, especially when it came to S's and soft C's (because the word I had trouble with in the incident in class was 'something').

My brothers seemed to shake their stutters by the time they got to secondary school, whereas mine became an integral part of my personality. I attached a lot of importance to the ability to communicate effectively, so because I wasn't able to do this, I had low self-esteem, low self-worth and low self-image. I also had a lower tolerance for things not going my way, was very sensitive to criticism and had zero resilience. I adopted strategies to reduce stuttering to avoid potential criticism; the main strategy was to not talk at all.

Writing became a sanctuary: I found comfort in being able to express myself exactly how I wanted to when I wrote. It always felt like I was only being 40 per cent of my authentic self when I was with other people, but writing allowed me to unlock that other elusive 60 per cent.

I chose to go into admin work after leaving school because it seemed to better fit my more introverted temperament. I thought this work would involve less verbal communication than other jobs, but it meant on a daily basis I had to face my archnemesis – the dreaded telephone.

I don't mean to paint a picture of constant doom and gloom because it wasn't all bad. The benefits of introversion included being more introspective. When I was older, I discovered a life-changing psychological idea that seemed unique. It explained why we have negative emotions – one of the biggest obstacles to resilience. We'll discuss this idea in Chapter 4.

I threw myself into studying the mind and read as many books as I could. I thought about becoming a therapist but was held back by the fact that none of the theories and techniques I had learnt had resolved my stutter – I couldn't reconcile the idea of helping people with their issues when I couldn't help myself with mine. However, I continued reading books as an area of keen personal interest.

After working mainly in admin jobs for various companies, I ended up working for a local authority in north London for twenty years. On my commute from south London, I entertained myself by either reading or playing games on a portable gaming device. One day I saw an advert for an app alleging it could teach anyone how to draw in a few simple steps. I thought that unlikely, but as I had nothing to lose except maybe a bit of time, I thought I'd give it a go.

After a few lessons, my efforts were suspiciously good – I thought the device must be tricking me. I decided to copy something I drew on the device onto some paper and realized I was already much better than I ever thought I could be. This was a revelation. I grew up wishing I could draw but it seemed like it was a talent that eluded me, despite many attempts. I grew up with three close friends who could all draw very well, but every time I tried my efforts were laughable in comparison, so I stuck to what I was better at: writing.

Through learning how to draw I unknowingly developed a growth mindset – a concept that I will cover in Chapter 6. I believed if I could learn how to draw, I could potentially learn anything. I attended a one-day coaching course, which explained to me what a growth mindset was. One of my colleagues left to become a solicitor soon after. That made me realize that I had a growth mindset for most things, but a fixed mindset about my career and my speech. Until then, I was more than happy to remain in office jobs my entire working life and thought my speech was always going to be an obstacle of some kind.

I questioned what new career I might embark on and remembered that, years before, I had wanted to become a therapist. I reframed my past and realized that I was actually more communicative than I had previously allowed myself to believe. I started to remember lots of incidents where my stutter had either been very minor or non-existent. I realized I had more resilience than I was giving myself credit for, because I had pushed myself to go to social events or to do other things that were outside my comfort zone. A lot of those things hadn't gone as well as I hoped they would, but I continued to show up to similar social events.

I also reframed that initial event when my classmates laughed at me. Back then, I often made my classmates laugh on purpose, so when I allowed myself to try to remember that fateful event in more detail, I realized it wasn't the whole class but only some of my classmates that laughed at me – a third at most – and it was much more likely they were intending to laugh *with* me rather than *at* me.

These new insights prompted another realization: my speech might not be the impenetrable barrier I thought it was. I explored a few counselling course options, and signed up for a three-year diploma that included hypnotherapy and basic counselling skills. In the final year, I undertook two coaching courses. After qualifying, I specialized in helping people understand and deal with emotions generally, as well as anxiety, trauma, depression and self-esteem issues in particular. Since then, I have been developing my own approach based on a few existing ones and philosophical ideas, along with my own discoveries interwoven with neuroscience. With this approach, as well as a few other fundamental principles, I have helped clients navigate a wide range of challenging situations.

What Resilience Isn't ... & What It Is

With that context provided, let us return to the topic of resilience. In 2022, I began working as a group facilitator with a project that provided therapeutic support for the NHS (the UK's health service) staff. One of the more interesting discussions we had was defining what resilience was. The group members were all in extremely challenging situations. The consensus was that the word 'resilience' had been weaponized by senior colleagues they had grievances with; some members of staff had been told they weren't resilient enough. So, 'resilience' in this context seemed to mean staff not challenging the status quo, allowing themselves to be a walkover or accepting something that would not be in their best interests to accept. Numbness to a challenging situation is another example of what resilience isn't, because the word 'numbness' usually suggests a sense of resignation or powerlessness.

The Oxford English Dictionary defines resilience as the capacity to withstand or recover quickly from difficulties.[1] So, resilience can be broken down into two parts: withstanding and recovering. Through history, stories of the human spirit have proven countless times that the mind and the body have an innate capacity to do both, unless they are impeded. These impediments can be understood and navigated.

The purpose of this book is to help you experience a state of consistent resilience to the point where it becomes habitual. We will cover a lot of ground, combining aspects of psychology, philosophy, history, science and human interest. Our species has collectively demonstrated resilience for over 200,000 years, which has brought us to the modern day. The recent challenges we have faced with the COVID-19 pandemic and other global crises have helped to shape our current view of resilience. It's fair to say that in recent years, most of us have experienced direct, and sometimes continuous, evidence that in a lot of ways we are more resilient than we may have thought we were.

CHAPTER ONE

Quick Tips to Rebuild Resilience

Our view of resilience stems from our thoughts about it. Our thoughts matter. If we believe we can't do something, we haven't just made it impossible to do that thing – though it might seem impossible – but we have probably made it a lot harder. The subject of mindsets will be explored in more detail later in the book, but I will introduce them in this chapter by describing just how much impact our thoughts have on our experience. This highlights how powerful our thoughts are – or, to be more specific, how much power we give to them.

The Power of Thoughts

A thought is a product of thinking, and thinking can take any shape. It's the production or organization of any type of data that can be linked to any of the five senses or to our stream of consciousness.

Some thoughts are motivational. If you have the thought, 'I'm hungry', you could find yourself automatically going to get some food. If you have the thought, 'Go and get some food!', you may be more easily motivated because you're giving yourself something that sounds more like a command. At the same time, however, you could repeatedly entertain the thought, 'Go and get some food!' and do nothing. You have the power to defuse or ignore the thought because it's just a thought.

Thoughts only have the power that we give to them. They're not reality or compelling commands, even though we often treat them like they are. There's a part of the brain, the thalamus, which often causes us to treat thoughts as if they are commands, so we act accordingly.

A specific thought, no matter what it is, isn't the most important part of the experience. What is more important is how we react to it. The thought stems from a subconscious process, so a process we may not be aware of consciously. How we respond to it is also often a subconscious process. This can be clearly demonstrated if we consider how three people could have three different reactions to the same thought.

ONE STEP AT A TIME

This chapter will describe several different ways of rebuilding resilience quickly. You may find it useful initially to pick one or two of these ideas and focus on them before looking at the others. This will mean you stand a greater chance of becoming more proficient in those areas more quickly. You can then incorporate some of the other ideas into your life later.

Same Thought, Different Reactions

Let's meet Leo, Jenny and Taylor, who have the same thought in the same situation about an imminent presentation.

Negative Confirmation Bias

First, Leo, has the thought, 'I'm going to fail'. He accepts this thought and instantly believes it. He might believe it for a self-reinforcing and circular reason – why would he be having the thought if it wasn't true? The thought gains more traction the more it's entertained, and this has a profound effect on Leo's consequent thoughts and behaviour. It activates a negative confirmation bias, which means Leo only remembers events that didn't go well and doesn't remember events that did go well. Soon, and maybe understandably by this stage, Leo is convinced of his belief, and delivering a bad presentation feels like a looming inevitability.

Leo has now increased the chances of not doing well because of how he reacted to the thought. He's pinning a lot of importance on this representation. His feelings are attached to the projected outcome and he feels negatively because he's convinced the presentation is going to go badly. He believes if it goes wrong, it could have serious consequences on his career and life generally. He sees his performance as a direct reflection of his capability and character. He places massive demands on himself and believes he has zero margin for error.

So, it's understandable that Leo feels a significant amount of stress when he thinks about the presentation. The thought of it going wrong could prompt him to spiral into an intensely negative state that might be difficult to recover from. He has a fixed idea about how resilient he is.

Neutral Bias

The second person, Jenny, has the same thought, 'I'm going to fail'. But, unlike Leo, she questions it. A neutral bias follows, and she remembers past successes as well as other times when presentations didn't go quite as well as she hoped they would. Jenny may believe there's an equal chance of delivering a bad presentation, a mediocre one or a good one. Even with just two options of good or bad, Jenny acknowledges the chances of an ambiguous or a 50/50 outcome. She has an ambivalent view about how important the presentation is and feels reasonably resilient, so is fairly confident that no matter what happens, she'll cope with it. She attaches her feelings to the effort she imagines she will put into it. She plans to put in a lot of effort and so will be able to reduce her stress so it doesn't impact her views about her performance.

Positive Confirmation Bias

The third person, Taylor, has the exact same thought, 'I'm going to fail', but instead of accepting or questioning it, they outright refute it. They consider what they may have to do to prevent the presentation from going wrong. They think about doing additional preparation and practice and they put conscious effort into trying harder. This process could activate a positive confirmation bias, and they're spurred on by reminding themselves of successes in the past. This confirmation bias doesn't involve just thinking about times when presentations went well – they're not being delusional; they also remember times when things didn't go well, but they're more likely to think about those times in an objective or helpful way.

For example, there may have been mitigating circumstances to explain a presentation not going well, such as not having much time to prepare. They may also remember times when things didn't go well but they can think back to what happened and realize that every time this occurred, they learnt something, so increased the chances of things going better next time. Taylor will be confident that there's a higher chance of this presentation going well – or if it doesn't, that they will more than likely learn something from it.

Taylor thinks about the event objectively, considering the bigger picture. They acknowledge that the company would prefer that it goes well, so the presentation is important to them in that respect, but they think about it within the context of other things in their life and don't place too much personal importance on it. They would prefer it goes well, but accept the possibility that it might not. Taylor's feelings are attached to the fact they're able to give the presentation in the first place, as this is an excellent opportunity for personal and professional development.

Make the Subconscious, Conscious

Let's imagine the presentation didn't go as well as hoped for any of them, and they receive feedback reflecting this. Leo is likely to take that as a criticism of his character and will probably shy away from future endeavours in an understandable effort to protect his ego. His view of resilience is now worse than it was. Jenny identifies presentations as an area for improvement to work on to promote her professional development. Her view of resilience remains intact. Taylor also identifies presentations as an area for improvement in a way that reinforced their previous stance. If it goes wrong, what can they learn from it? They don't see it as a flaw in character or a mark on their level of competence. Their resilience has increased, and they see the benefit of putting themselves forward for future opportunities.

You could admire the way Taylor thinks but quite rightly acknowledge that you're not them. This is true, but you can think in a similar way, and if you do this, you increase the chances of achieving similar results. If you catch yourself thinking like Leo, you can ask yourself, what do I need to do to think more like Jenny? Once you're more comfortable entertaining those thoughts, you might find yourself more often thinking like Taylor. Although thinking stems from a subconscious process, we can bring this subconscious process into conscious awareness, and consciously act rather than continuing to automatically respond.

Acceptance & Self-compassion

As described earlier in the chapter, Leo found himself attaching his performance and resilience levels to his self-image. One way to resolve self-image issues is to nurture a mindset of acceptance and self-compassion. If we don't accept ourselves, we're creating a dissonance between what's there and what we want to be there.

To presuppose something is to naturally and effortlessly assume it's true. Rather than asking *if* we're going shopping on Saturday, it's asking *what time* on Saturday are we going shopping? Rather than wondering *are we* going to go to a certain shop, you can ask are we going to spend *five minutes* or *ten minutes* there? A simple presupposition technique is to use the word 'yet', as it naturally implies that something *will* happen, it's just a matter of time.

Our thoughts about ourselves are usually rigid and often non-compassionate. A recurring theme for a lot of people I speak to is the apparent norm of them being unquestioningly and genuinely compassionate to other people, while being unable to direct compassion inward.

A common reason for this is the view that self-compassion is a gateway to self-indulgence. People think that having that extra biscuit is a slippery slope and, soon enough, they'll be eating a whole packet of biscuits every day. That's an example of black and white thinking. If you entertain A, you will jump to Z rather than stopping at a letter on the way. This is not necessarily true and, even if it were, surely experiencing the benefits of self-indulgence is preferable to experiencing the forced austerity of self-neglect.

The reason why some people feel apprehensive about self-compassion is understandable, but I haven't heard anyone express concern over their kindness for other people mutating into over-indulgence to the point where they have to be mean to that person as a preventative measure.

Demands Versus Preferences

A lot of our views about ourselves come from the demands we place on ourselves. Rational Emotive Behaviour Therapy (REBT), the original form of Cognitive Behaviour Therapy (CBT), addresses this by explaining that our emotions stem from our beliefs, and our beliefs can either be rigid and false, or true and flexible. A demand is an example of a rigid, false belief. A preference is a flexible, true belief.

If you have a *demand* about resilience – 'I must be resilient', – and you're not resilient, you're going to be disturbed and that can contribute to a sense of low self-esteem. That will significantly decrease the chances of you being resilient because you won't be feeling resourceful. The result of a demand not being met often seems catastrophic because demands are imperatives – they're universal laws that must be always adhered to, hence they're false beliefs. It is not true that things *must* happen because you demand them to.

The *preference* equivalent might be, 'I would prefer if I was more resilient, but I accept that I may not be in certain situations'. If you're resilient straight away, great; but if you are not, you may be upset but you won't be disturbed. When you're upset and not disturbed, you're more resourceful, so you'll be more likely to work out what you need to do in order to be more resilient, and you're more likely to make those changes. Unmet demands can lead to catastrophic thoughts and unbearable feelings towards yourself, others or the world, for example, thoughts of 'I'm a failure' or 'Other people are rubbish' or 'The world is cold and unfair'.

Using preferences instead of demands increases the chances of you being flexible and open to change. Unmet preferences may still lead to negative thoughts, but those negative thoughts will have a limit; you may think the situation is bad, but you can acknowledge that it's not the end of the world. That will result in uncomfortable but bearable feelings, which can ultimately lead to universal acceptance – accepting yourself, others and the world: 'I'm fallible and that's okay' or 'Other people may not respond in a way I want them to and that's okay. That doesn't mean the world is an unfair place'. One of the trickier things to accept about the idea of self-acceptance is that it should be universal and unconditional.

Reimagining Stress

How much stress we feel usually has a direct impact on how resilient we are. The more stress we feel, the less resilience we are able to access, which is ironic since we surely benefit from having more resilience during times of stress.

Positive & Negative Stress

Stress is a very common emotion but despite that, it's usually not very well understood. For starters, there are two types of stress: distress and eustress. Distress is what people are usually referring to when they're talking about stress. Eustress is its less-known positive counterpart. Usually, feeling eustress leads to positive responses. It has been referred to as a challenge-based response, instead of a threat-based response.

It's a common belief that we need to stress to function or excel. If that is the case, it might be true for eustress but not for distress, although people are often thinking about distress when they make this claim.

Motivation & Stress

People often say that they need stress to motivate them; this isn't true. You can feel stressed and motivated, but that doesn't mean that you can't be motivated without feeling stress.

There's a similar idea to the path of least resistance called the law of reversed effort. This is the idea that the amount of effort we put into something actually decreases the chances of getting that thing. An example of this is going to an interview. You could put pressure on yourself because of how much you want the job, but that pressure could cause stress and that stress will impact on your interview performance. Under stress, you could be asked a simple question and struggle to find the answer. If you're more relaxed, you will have a more effective memory.

When I've shared this idea with some people, they've said something like, 'Well you need to make some effort'. This is true, you have to make some effort or there's no point attending the interview. But if you keep this law in mind, you'll ensure you're not making *too much* effort, because too much effort will be counterproductive.

The Four Pillars of Stress

Stress arises due to a narrative that involves a general perception of pressure, such as working to a short deadline or being told the results of your work will affect a lot of other people. But, along with this perception of pressure, three other things need to be happening at the same time for you to feel stress. We can call these four things together the pillars of stress. Understanding these pillars can help to manage and reduce the intensity of further negative emotions and improve performance. Let's take a look at them in more detail.

1. The first pillar is an overestimation of the amount of pressure that you're currently under. You might be feeling an 8 out of 10 amount of pressure, but in reality, it's only a 4

or 5 out of 10. The level of stress that you're feeling is directly linked to the amount of pressure you think you're under. If you realize you aren't under that much pressure, the stress will instantly reduce.

2. The second pillar is underestimating your ability to cope with the task or situation. If you accurately perceive the level of pressure but believe the task is one that you can achieve, you won't feel so stressed; you will more than likely get on with the things that you need to do in order to complete the task or make the most of the situation in the best way possible.
3. The third pillar is underestimating the chances of being assisted with the task or situation. If you accurately perceive the level of pressure and accurately believe you can't complete the task or deal with the situation yourself, but know you will get support, you will be less likely to feel stress and more likely to lean into the support.
4. The final pillar is overestimating the importance of the task. Importance is usually relative. When someone says something needs to be done, it usually means someone *wants* it to be done. How important is this task in the big picture? Is someone going to die if you don't achieve it? Most people are in jobs where other peoples' lives aren't hanging in the balance. To the people who have careers where life and death *is* a consideration, whether it's ever-present or occasional, most people are aware of the benefits of remaining as calm as possible. If you remain calm, you're less likely to make mistakes.

Reducing Stress

Even if you work on removing just one of these four pillars, your stress will reduce and that will increase your productivity. Once your productivity increases and you see that you have more control, that's often an incentive to make more changes, so your productivity will increase further.

For example, we can revisit the first pillar by asking where is the pressure coming from? If you realize that the pressure is coming from just yourself, you can reduce it. You may temporarily believe that you need stress to motivate you but then remind yourself that you don't need stress. Being able to work well under pressure doesn't mean that you need pressure to work well.

Mental Rehearsal

Mental rehearsal is sometimes referred to as visualization. Studies have shown that merely imagining scenarios has a profound effect on the brain.

One of the better-known studies into mental rehearsal involved a basketball team in an American university. Researchers split the players into three groups and recorded the success rate of their free throws. The first group were encouraged to practise making free throws for an hour each day. The second group just visualized themselves making free throws for an hour each day. The third group neither practised nor imagined practising.

The visualization group were instructed to imagine their throws in detail. They were asked to visualize in the first-person – so, to see what they would see with their own eyes if they were actually practising. They were encouraged to focus on the different sensory elements, for example, feeling the ball as they held it with one hand and steadied it with the other preparing to throw, seeing the basket and approximating the distance between it and the ball, feeling their muscles contracting as they took the shot, feeling the ball roll from their hand and seeing it launch into the air in a perfect trajectory, and then hearing the momentary sound of contact between the ball and the rim, followed by the satisfying sound of the ball rushing through the net.

After thirty days, each group was asked to take free throws. It wasn't surprising that the rate of baskets scored by the group that practised in the gym went up, by 24 per cent. It also wasn't surprising that the group that didn't practise at all didn't improve. The surprise came from how much the scores of the visualization group increased by: 23 per cent. Other researchers have replicated the results of this study, and it is now commonly recognized that mental rehearsal or visualization improves performance.

Lots of people use this technique either consciously or unconsciously when they're preparing for things like interviews. If you imagine being asked a certain question before an interview, and you are then asked that question, you won't feel put on the spot and will be able to answer it in a similar way as to when you mentally practised it.

Seeing Is Believing

Neuroscience can explain this phenomenon. Throughout the course of this book, I will refer often to several parts of the brain, including the neocortex, the thalamus and the prefrontal cortex. Let's find out a little about them.

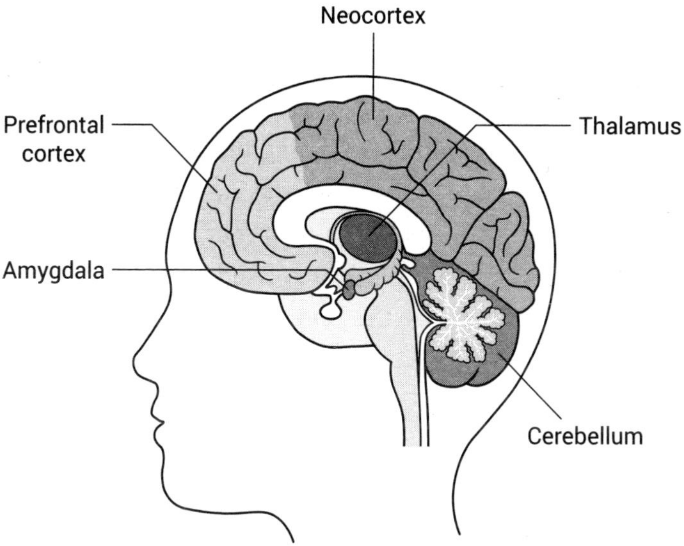

Figure 1: The human brain

- **Neocortex:** The neocortex is the outermost part of the brain, covering the whole of the main structure. It is activated when we imagine anything or think anything. The neocortex is connected to many other parts of the brain, including a structure in the middle called the thalamus.

- **Thalamus:** This is the brain's relay station – a bit like the postal department of an office. It receives information from many different parts of the brain and redirects this information to other parts of the brain so we respond in the most optimal way. But, the thalamus is unable to distinguish between thoughts that are based in reality and thoughts that are purely fantasy-based. To the thalamus, seeing is believing.
- **Prefrontal cortex:** The prefrontal cortex is the part of the brain that governs reason. It should kick in to regulate the thalamus.

Our emotional responses are based on ideas, not reality. The downside of this is that we can upset ourselves with thoughts about things that might not ever come true. The thalamus is responsible for Leo spiralling when he initially entertains thoughts of not giving an ideal or even a passable presentation; in his mind, he has already failed or he's in the process of failing. The upside, though, is that we can use our imagination as a training ground of infinite possibilities, through mental rehearsal.

This aspect of brain functioning means that if you imagine – visualize – that you're able to be more resilient, it will lead to you becoming more resilient. This won't necessarily convert into you actually getting what you want, but at least you've done what you can to tip the balance in your favour and increase the chances of this. If you have difficulty not feeling stress in certain situations, try to visualize how you would like to feel in that scenario.

The Illusion of Better

This is a good point to pause for a moment and think about the question, 'What motivates you the most?' Try to think of up to five answers.

If one hundred people were asked this question, you would probably hear recurring answers that include those you may have just thought of or written down. We would see money, success, self-improvement, family and other common relatable responses, and these are all effective conscious motivators. It would be sensible to consciously prioritize enjoyment over prestige and security over enjoyment, but there's a distinct possibility that we are all *unconsciously* motivated by something else.

It seems we are all unconsciously *more* motivated by the idea of 'better'. I don't mean self-improvement; I mean when one option is seen to be better than another option.

Let's consider someone who has identified security as their best motivator. If they were presented with two choices of how to best achieve security, they would choose what they believe to be the better option. Even if there was just one option, they would still make the supposedly better choice of doing that thing over not doing that thing

But that is not all there is to it; there's something else to consider. Often the *idea* of better is actually the *illusion* of better, because details of the choices you're presented with haven't been made explicit.

Illusion Versus Reality

To highlight the subconscious strategy underpinning this process, let's consider the example of anxiety. If someone experiences anxiety and they have the choice to avoid something or engage with it, they will usually choose avoidance, because of the discomfort levels they associate with engaging. The choice here can be boiled down to 'comfort' or 'discomfort', so choosing comfort (in the form of avoidance) makes sense, because we are biologically predisposed to go towards comfort and move ourselves away from discomfort.

It is true that avoidance provides comfort for people who experience anxiety, but it arguably results in just a slight and temporary reduction in their anxiety, so only provides temporary comfort. In most cases, avoidance actually prolongs the anxiety, because if someone experiences discomfort but gets used to it, the discomfort reduces. Long-term comfort is actually more likely if that person were to engage with their anxiety. If the choice of 'comfort' is shown within the context of the bigger picture, it may not seem as appealing. By acknowledging the long-term effects of avoidance we can expose the illusion.

The illusion is easier to see once we expand the choices to demonstrate the consequences. While it seems we have the simple choice between comfort or discomfort, we're actually deciding between:

1. Immediate, temporary, minor comfort but delayed, prolonged and major ***discomfort***
2. Immediate, temporary, minor discomfort but delayed, prolonged and major ***comfort***

If we look at the choices in more detail, 'comfort' becomes less appealing, as through avoidance anxiety is retained and we see it is just discomfort in disguise, and 'discomfort' becomes more appealing, as through engagement anxiety is resolved and the discomfort is just a precursor to prolonged comfort. This can be summarized as a choice between short-term gain and long-term pain versus short-term pain and long-term gain.

This won't apply to everybody and every case of being resilient. We might choose not to be resilient because of the potential negative consequences. We think that being resilient means we are promoting negative outcomes or that we're condoning less than ideal behaviour. These negative consequences could be real or illusory.

However, even if we know that our perceived negative outcomes are indeed illusory, even if we are aware of the real choice before us and know what feels like the right thing to do, we might still feel compelled to choose an unhelpful path. This may indicate a trauma response of some kind. Trauma will be covered in Chapters 6, 7 and 8. Another form of the illusion of better will be explained in Chapter 5.

The Solution-focused Approach

People are usually in two camps when it comes to how effective positive thinking is. I'm on the less enamoured side. I point out to my clients the benefits of trying to think rationally rather than trying to think positively.

The first self-help book I read was called *Psycho-Cybernetics*, written in 1960 by Maxwell Maltz.[2] It was one of the first books that demonstrated the power of positive thinking.

Yet, positive thinking may have drawbacks that eclipse the benefits. If you use positive thinking alone, and think things are going to work out and everything's going to be fine, you may neglect to do practical things to increase the chances of this positive outcome.

The *rational* approach is to think, 'No matter how things turn out, I'm going to make the most of the situation'. If things go to plan, make the most of it. If things don't go to plan, try to deal with it in the best way possible. I believe a more realistic form of positivity will ensue if you think rationally;

you could focus on practical things you need to do to increase the chances of getting the outcome you want.

Focus on What You Want

In his book, Maltz describes two principles of the subconscious mind. These are the agreement principle and the compliance principle. The agreement principle is the idea that the subconscious always agrees with what the conscious mind tells it. The compliance principle extends this and states your subconscious actually moves you to act in the direction of what the conscious mind tells it.

Again, this is thalamus territory. If you have a thought, the first item on the agenda is to give that thought a sense of concreteness rather than challenging it. If you think you're not resilient, the brain scrambles for a way to prove you right.

These two principles help describe the foundation for a type of therapy that lots of people find effective. It's called the Solution-focused Brief Therapy approach. A lot of the time we think in a problem-saturated way. If we're in a situation that we don't like, it's easy to focus on what's going wrong and the negative way it's impacting us. This leads to less resourceful states – we can feel drained and exhausted, and experience additional negative emotions that won't help our efforts.

If we instead focus on what is going right and/or what we want instead of what we're currently getting, we will more than likely feel more positive emotions. That will lead to a more resourceful state, when we feel more energized and in a better position to more effectively solve the issue or get what we want.

When I started to learn more about the brain, one of the ideas that appealed to me was that of 'maximal direction'. This is similar to the compliance principle, but it makes clear that the brain doesn't just provide one route to get you to your desired outcome, it automatically provides as many routes as possible. It's like the brain has a hidden satnav feature. The idea of where you want to be is the destination; the routes are the things we may need to do to reach it.

If you have a clear idea of where you want to be and a good idea of where you are now, the subconscious mind will usually easily and automatically do the rest unless the conscious mind gets in the way. This automatic process can be facilitated by thinking about what the obstacles are and removing them, thereby creating more paths of least resistance.

We tend to get more of what we think about, and the brain has difficulty processing negative words like 'don't and 'can't'. If you're trying to not do something, you might be indirectly making it harder for yourself. If I said to you, 'Don't think of a pink elephant', there's a strong chance you're going to start thinking of a pink elephant. Even though I'm clearly saying, '*Don't* think of a pink elephant' the brain interprets that as '*Think* of a pink elephant' because it has difficulty processing the word 'don't'. It's almost like it has to first do the thing you're saying not to do to before it can try to work out how to not do it.

Transferring Skills

When someone identifies resilience as a state they want to achieve or improve, I always initially ask them to describe what being more resilient looks like. Sometimes the person doesn't know, or they describe a behaviour they already exhibit. That means they're resilient in some areas of their lives but not in others.

Transferring skills from one area of your life to another is an often-used solution-focused technique. Most people are resilient in some areas of their life but not in others. You might find yourself being effortlessly resilient at work, dealing with clients or colleagues, but find it a struggle when you're dealing with family members in certain scenarios. If you can be resilient in one area of your life, the chances are you can be more resilient in another if you use a similar strategy. If you're more resilient at work, you're being so because you think that's the better decision. When you're not resilient at home, you're being so because you think that's the better decision, but you can explore why and focus on the short-term and long-term consequences.

Mindfulness

We tend to spend a lot of time in the past and the future, rather than focusing on the present, which may involve neglecting it. Rather than criticizing ourselves for past mistakes, we can learn from them; if we focus on the present in a more meaningful way, the chances of making the most of the present and having a better future are increased. This is a much healthier and more helpful approach than criticizing ourselves because of the past and worrying about the future.

Mindfulness in some form has existed for thousands of years – it appears in several popular religions – but it has seen a resurgence over the last couple of decades. It's a type of meditation that focuses on the present without judgement.

One way of doing this is to imagine your thoughts and feelings as being a powerful waterfall. We usually stand directly underneath this waterfall, which means we can't help but be affected by all our thoughts and feelings. But if you imagine you are standing on a ledge just behind the waterfall, you can watch the water go by and are less likely to be swept away by it. When you start practising mindfulness you may find it difficult to not focus on the water, but when you notice yourself doing that, bring your focus back to yourself on the ledge merely observing the water. This can help you to accept the now, rather than struggling against it.

This is an example of a defusing technique. Defusing techniques help you detach from your thoughts and feelings

BOX BREATHING

You can relax by using a breathing technique called box breathing. There are four basic steps:

1. Breathe in through your nose, while counting slowly. A count of four or five is usually enough to induce a state of increased relaxation.
2. Hold your breath for the same count.
3. Breathe out through your mouth for the same count.
4. Hold your breath for the same count before breathing in again.

You could also escalate the count, so start with a count of four, but then on the second round increase this to a count of five, and so on. You may be able to get to a count of ten, or you might find it more comfortable stopping at a lower number.

in a healthy way. If you detach, you can then choose which thoughts and feelings to give more weight to rather than giving them all equal weight just because you're thinking or feeling them.

Mindfulness encourages you to adopt a third-person perspective rather than a first-person one. A first-person experience is an in-body experience, where you're sensing information first-hand, whereas a third-person experience is an out-of-body experience, where you're looking at yourself sensing the information. Certain experiences can seem overwhelming from the first-person view but are a lot less intense from a third-person view.

It's easy to become our thoughts if we overly attach to them. You're probably going to feel differently if you think, 'I *think* I'm not resilient' rather than 'I *am* not resilient'.

Mindfulness has multiple benefits. By its nature, it helps with attention because your mind is focused on certain aspects of the now. It can help you regulate your emotions better. It can also help you deal with challenging situations and the challenging thoughts and feelings that are often prompted. It also has benefits in terms of helping you maintain relationships more easily, because you're more likely to be empathetic towards other people. Finally, it can help you improve your sleep because you'll be generally more relaxed.

Sleep Hygiene

Your resilience is connected to your physical health. When you're feeling better physically, things are generally easier and this includes being naturally more resilient. Lots of studies have shown that getting a good night's sleep has a big impact on your physical health, so this section will focus on helping you improve your sleep hygiene.

Reset Your Body Clock

If we are mindful of our circadian rhythms – our body's response to a 24-hour cycle – we can manage our sleep better.

You can give yourself a reset by exposing yourself to fifteen to thirty minutes of daylight before noon; studies have shown that even sitting by a window can be beneficial. Your body uses this exposure to daylight to help calculate how long it needs to be awake for. Ensure you're protected from UV rays by wearing appropriate sun protection, and never look directly at the sun.

Food & Drink Curfew

Try to not eat too close to bedtime. If you leave at least three hours between having food and going to bed, your circadian rhythms won't be affected. If you don't leave this amount of time, you're potentially going to find it harder to fall asleep. The same goes for liquids, although one or two hours is usually enough time for your body to process excess water so that your sleep is not interrupted by needing the bathroom.

Restrict Screen Time

Looking at screens before going to bed disrupts your circadian rhythms. Try to stop looking at screens at least half an hour before going to sleep. If you do look at screens, dim the brightness or use a nighttime mode if your electronic device has one.

Try to Relax

We find it easier to fall asleep when we cease all activity. When you're unable to fall asleep, trying to fall asleep *is* activity. Instead of trying to fall asleep, try to relax.

The more relaxed you are, the more likely you are to drift off. You can relax by focusing on your breathing (see box, page 37). This can be combined with mindfulness to ground you in the moment so that you're not thinking about the past or the future.

Count

Counting sheep used to be the go-to method of distracting your mind to help you fall asleep. It works in a similar way to part of a hypnotic induction, by distracting the conscious mind so that the subconscious can naturally do what it's designed to do, in this case, drift off into sleep. You don't have to count sheep; just try counting backwards from a thousand, which is a technique that some hypnotherapists use to induce or deepen a hypnotic trance.

Deal With Problem Thoughts

Some people find it challenging to go to sleep because this time of day is when we find ourselves ruminating. Ruminating is when our brain gets stuck in a cycle of negative thoughts – it is trying to solve a problem but in a less than ideal way.

Rather than entertaining a constant carousel of repetitive, unhelpful thoughts, give yourself a limited amount of time to think about an issue. Ask yourself, what am I trying to resolve here? Is there anything I can do, or do I have to wait and see what happens? A lot of the time we're worrying about an event that we have no control over. I was very familiar with the phrase 'I'll cross that bridge when I come to it'. There then came a point when I realized that most bridges don't exist, and I was worrying about something that I didn't need to be. You can pre-empt that future realization by acknowledging now that you may be worrying about nothing.

What Ifs …

Often our rumination takes a particular form: what ifs. What ifs are often open cans of worms. An effective way to resolve a 'what if' is to treat it as if it's a question, and then answer the question. This closes the can and helps you focus on practical actions you can take if the event you're worrying about does actually take place. 'What if I miss my train tomorrow?' 'I'd catch the next one or catch another train and go an alternate route'.

A lot of 'what ifs' are worst-case scenarios. You can amend the process and ask yourself, 'In the *unlikely event* that such and such happens, what would I do?' Then answer the question with an 'even if': 'Even if such and such happens, I will cope by doing this.'

The thalamus makes all 'what ifs' real as soon as we imagine them. Answering the question or replacing 'what ifs' with 'even ifs' engages the prefrontal cortex – the part of the brain that uses reason to regulate the thalamus.

If Only …

'If only' can be considered the retrospective version of 'what if'. 'What ifs' are about potential future events; 'if onlys' are focused on things that have already happened that you wanted to happen differently. You may torture yourself because an event didn't go the way you wanted it to. Using the 'even if' technique is a good way to resolve these ruminations. *Even if* you did something different, you still may not have got the result that you wanted. You would just be in a slightly different situation, with another 'if only' as a potential source of upset. This could go on indefinitely. Rather than struggling against the past, accept it and plan to make the most of things as healthily and as authentically as possible.

Key Takeaways

- Our thoughts have only the power we give them, so we can respond to them however we want.
- Self-compassion enables resilience.
- We can reimagine stress by focusing on the four pillars – reducing any of them will reduce stress.
- Mentally rehearsing can help us become more resilient.
- When we make choices, we often fall for the illusion of better because we aren't aware of long-term consequences.
- Be present in the moment without judgement.
- Improving your sleep will increase resilience.

CHAPTER TWO

The Fundamentals of Reality

Understanding philosophy can be impactful as it provides fundamental concepts around which our understanding of life is based. This chapter will demonstrate how adopting one approach – Stoicism – can immediately help us regain resilience. We will also explore a model of perception that can make it easier for us to perceive in a more objective way. Finally, we'll focus on the power of narratives and the link between our narratives and our emotions. Just by considering some of these ideas, we can start to nurture a sense of increased resilience.

Stoicism

The word 'Stoicism' is often confused with the word 'stoic'. Being stoic generally means not showing emotion, whereas Stoicism is an ancient Greek philosophy.

Stoicism highlights the impact that our beliefs have on our experiences and emotions. It suggests that we should be aiming to lead the best lives we can, while ensuring our beliefs are as rational as possible. Some of the descriptions of Stoicism sound like descriptions of resilience.

Stoicists realized that we could lead happier lives if we accepted reality rather than struggled against it. Rather than feeling bad about something that won't change, Stoicism asks us to consider what practical thing can we do to feel better about the situation or make the most of it. It presupposes resilience, and one way to effortlessly achieve something is to presuppose it.

This general attitude of acceptance shows up in many areas. It is typified in a commonly recited piece of text called the Serenity Prayer. The origin of the prayer has been contested, with two different attributed authors, Reinhold Niebuhr and Winnifred Wygal. The most common version we see today was first published in 1951. The prayer starts with '*God* grant me the serenity … ' but when I recite the prayer I usually remove the word 'God' so more people can relate to it.

The whole prayer consists of two sentences, but it is the first sentence that is more commonly recited: ' … grant me the serenity to accept the things I can't change, the courage to change the things I can and the wisdom to know the difference.'[3] This makes explicit that we can influence how we view things by distinguishing between the things we can control and the things we can't. Stoicists pointed out that we tend to disturb ourselves when negative events happen by having unhealthy beliefs about those bad events. Whether events happen or not are often beyond our control but we can control how we respond to them.

Perception

It's generally accepted that we create our realities based on information received by our five main sensory receptors: our eyes, ears, skin, tongue and nose. These senses, along with information already held in our memory, help create a model of reality. This model is then projected outwards and our senses then perceive the model that we've just created.

Another way of saying this is there's one reality that we're in – the objective or universal reality, and this is the master copy or the goal of the subjective or individual realities we perceive.

REBT & NEGATIVE EMOTIONS

A psychologist called Albert Ellis started developing a psychotherapeutic approach called Rational Therapy in 1955. It is now known as Rational Emotive Behaviour Therapy (REBT).

REBT is the original form of Cognitive Behaviour Therapy (CBT), and challenges you to change your whole way of thinking. Once you delve deeply into the past or into a subconscious pattern or behaviour, you can apply a REBT way of looking at that thing in order to feel differently about it.

REBT suggests that there are only sixteen different negative emotions: eight unhealthy ones, and their healthy counterparts. It is believed that every other negative emotion stems from these sixteen base emotions.

The unhealthy negative emotions are:

- depression
- anxiety
- anger
- hurt
- shame
- guilt
- unhealthy envy
- unhealthy jealousy

Our subjective realities should always mirror the objective one, but because our subjective realities come from our senses, we can be fooled and mirror something that isn't there. If something has been mirrored, it's true and concrete

The healthy counterpart emotions are:

- sadness
- worry/concern
- frustration/annoyance
- disappointment
- regret
- remorse
- healthy envy
- healthy jealousy

The unhealthy negative emotions are sometimes referred to as 'stuck states', meaning if someone is feeling depressed, they usually find it difficult to be motivated, which means the state will more than likely persist. If you're feeling the healthier negative emotion of sadness instead, you're more likely to do things that increase the chances of lifting the sadness, like reach out to a friend, listen to music or go for a walk.

If something has happened to upset you, that thing may well be beyond your control, but with the help of REBT you can decide how you respond to it with acceptance. Instead of feeling depressed, you can feel sad; instead of feeling hurt, you can feel disappointed; instead of feeling anxious, you can feel concerned. REBT is a contemporary form of Stoicism.

to the person who mirrored it regardless of whether it's true objectively. This is why someone can have a belief about reality and another person can have a belief that completely opposes it, and both people can be convinced their view is the correct one. What this means is we don't believe things that are true; things are true because we believe them.

When I used to speak to people about this, I sometimes got tripped up because it seems our language wasn't designed to help explain this phenomenon. I could say 'belief is reality' to some people and they would understand what I meant. I would say it to other people and they would think I meant if someone believed something, it wouldn't just be real to them, it would be real to everyone, which clearly isn't the case. To navigate this truth minefield, the scientific method was created. If a methodical process is followed, the chances of believing in something that's more objective and less subjective is increased. The scientific method involves creating a hypothesis and then testing it, rather than having a belief and then blindly believing it because it seems true at the time.

Rotoscoping

I didn't have a way of easily explaining how we perceive until I came across an animation technique called rotoscoping. Most animation is done by drawing frames and then putting those frames together to make a cartoon. The result is usually a somewhat choppy style of animation. In the early 1900s, an animator created another form of animation. He realized he could get a much more realistic and fluid type of animation if he shot film and then drew frames by tracing over the film before putting the drawings together. The technique was called rotoscoping.

When I learnt about this style of animation, I realized it was a good way to describe our perception process. The film is objective reality and the cartoon is the world we see – our subjective realities. The cartoon is a product of our sensory impressions. It's impossible to see the actual film, because we're restricted to seeing our already drawn or copied cartoon version of it.

The idea is we would only trace the film and that should decrease the chance of rotoscoping something that isn't there. However, because of shortcuts our brains make, we don't have to use our senses to create reality, we can use other peoples' senses. This means we can rotoscope a reality based mainly on the words of someone we trust. If we rotoscope something based on someone else's senses, it will be as concrete to us as if we had directly experienced and copied the film ourselves.

We have so much control over this process that if the film contains something that contradicts the cartoon, our cartoon will often supersede the film. Rather than updating the cartoon so it is more in line with the film data, we reject the film data as false. An example of this is when you have an excellent reason to believe something is true, but when you try to convince another person they don't believe you. They're biased to their cartoon and not the film we're all trying to copy.

Past Narratives

Rotoscoping is just part of the perception process. If you were merely receiving information, the things you perceive wouldn't have any meaning; we also need a database that gives meanings to these objects. This database is all the things you've rotoscoped already. This includes past narratives. Some of these past stories are more important than others, and we build our worlds using them as foundations, such as religious, philosophical or spiritual ideas. In animation terms, this is the equivalent of continually rotoscoping a background.

We're going to examine different theories of emotion in Chapter 4. These theories are merely past narratives that other people have rotoscoped. We were introduced to them and we didn't challenge them because we accepted the person's authority and didn't have any reason to think the film contained something else.

We are all rotoscoping our current levels of resilience. We may not be rotoscoping objectively because of certain biases, but we can be aware of these biases and not let them influence us. We may think we're accurately seeing reality because of certain cues, but our perception creates a Catch-22, which is an escapable situation created by aspects of the situation. Belief is reality: if you believe something, it will be true to you; if you think you're resilient, you're right; if you think you're not resilient, you're also right.

The ACE Framework

Combining a few different psychological ideas, I have created a framework of perception and emotion called the ACE Framework. In this framework:

BIASES

We are potentially affected by biases at any time. The best way around this is to be aware of them, so we're not subconsciously influenced. Here are some common biases:

- CONFIRMATION BIAS: This is where we believe something and notice things that confirm that belief and ignore things that disconfirm it. If someone gets labelled with being non-punctual, people are more likely to notice or give relevance to times when they're late and not notice or give relevance to times when they're early or on time.
- PRIMARY BIAS: This is where we give more weight to the first version we see of something than we do to later versions. When you like the original of a film and see a remake, you're more likely to favour the original.
- NEGATIVITY BIAS: This is where we tend to give more weight to perceived negatives rather than perceived positives. This is why if ten people give feedback, and nine are positive and one is negative, we're likely to focus on the one negative rather than the nine positives.

- A = activating event
- C = concept. When we experience events, we create a narrative about the event and the important elements of that story can be boiled down to a concept.
- E = emotion

A lot of people have an A–E way of thinking. They think our emotions are caused by events, and the language they use demonstrates this – for example, 'My boss *made* me angry' or 'I was *left* feeling angry after speaking to my boss'.

If they had an A–C–E way of thinking, they would acknowledge the proactive part they're playing in their emotional response. This person would be more likely to say something like, 'My boss said something and I responded angrily to it'. The event or another person isn't prompting a particular response – the individual is responsible for prompting the response by how they're representing the event.

The activating event (A) doesn't lead to emotion (E); it's our interpretation or story of the event, particularly the boiled-down concept (C), that leads to the emotion. The event doesn't have direct impact on us – it's our interpretation of the event that has direct impact. Since our emotions stem from our specific perspective or interpretation, if we change our perspective or interpretation, our emotion will change.

I will often interchangeably use the words 'story', 'concept', 'interpretation' and 'perspective' to mean virtually the same thing. The ACE framework helps keep in mind that there is and always will be a separation between reality and our perception of it. This model makes clear that we are never going to see reality – we are only going to see our 'best guess' version of it, and this best guess often falls short of being as objective as it could be. This might be a hard pill to swallow for some, but this aspect of our experience means we have a lot more influence over our realities than we may have thought.

There's a quote from a Stoic philosopher named Epictetus that summarizes this: 'People are disturbed not by things, but by the views which they take of things.' We are often much more affected by our thoughts about events than we are by the events themself.

Merging the ACE framework with the quote looks like this: 'People are disturbed (E) not by things (A) but by the views (C) they take of things (A).' So it's not the A (activating event) that causes E (emotions), it's the C (concept/narrative) about the A that leads to E.

Controlling Our Reality

We won't have to remind ourselves that we are separated from reality by our interpretation of it after we've taken the idea onboard on an emotional level. Once we've done this, it will be a given. This understanding gives us more influence over our realities and highlights how much agency we have in any given situation.

It wouldn't be practical for us to recreate everything in reality so we minimize certain aspects of reality and maximize others by filtering the information we receive. We have complete creative licence over how these filters are used, but most of these filters are unconscious. We unconsciously try to create the best version of reality we can based on the data presented to us, but often, our version of reality is far from the best.

We have absolute authority over our realities because our stories overwrite what's there. You could say that every narrative we tell ourselves isn't the true story that we may have initially thought it was. Our narratives are *based* on true stories. A criticism of frameworks like this one is that

PRINCIPLES OF EMOTIONAL RESPONSIBILITY

There are two principles of emotional responsibility: the general principle and the specific principle. The general principle explains that in all situations, we are responsible for what we think, how we feel and how we behave. This contrasts with the apparently more common view: events are responsible for making us think, feel and behave in the way we do.

The general principle of emotional responsibility leads to the specific principle of emotional responsibility. The specific principle shows that we feel the way we do because of the beliefs we hold. An event could take place, and we could have a belief about the event that leads to a certain emotion. If another belief was held about that same event, it would lead to another emotion.

some people feel they are being blamed for their situation; I understand it might come across that way, depending on how this information is shared. Hopefully when the framework is shared, it's done so more from a place of empowerment.

Rotoscoping is an integral part of storytelling because it describes the mechanism that creates the story. When we understand that we are in control of how we perceive events, we can persuade ourselves to entertain only perspectives that presuppose resilience. We can think back to a time when we were effortlessly resilient. Then, we can look at similarities between that situation and our current one, which will help us feel just as resilient now as we did then. We can also entertain only thoughts that presuppose resilience. For example we can tell ourselves, 'I am in control of how resilient I am. Situations do not dictate my resilience levels.'

Why does all this matter? Our view of resilience could dramatically change just by acknowledging that the situation we are in isn't as important as our attitude towards the situation. It also matters because we often think things without knowing why. Unless we know what we're thinking and why, we stand a greater chance of being misled or misinterpreting something.

Key Takeaways

- Stoicism tells us we can't always control what happens to us, but we can control how we respond to it.
- We can use REBT to help us change unhealthy negative emotions into healthy negative emotions.
- Things mean what we say they mean – life only has the meaning we give to it.
- Certain thoughts presuppose resilience.
- Our perception is very similar to rotoscope animation – our version of reality is based on a master copy, but our copy overwrites the original.
- We are responsible for how we think, feel and behave.
- The ACE framework reminds us that our emotions directly stem from our narratives and not reality – and we can change our narratives.

CHAPTER THREE

Reframing

The narratives we tell ourselves are generated within our subconscious – our brains do this seamlessly. Yet, if we leave this job up to our subconscious, we will continue generating the narratives we have always done, and our view of resilience won't change. We can consciously intervene in this process and proactively change our perspective using a process called reframing. This chapter will look at three types of reframing: two common types that most people do automatically, and one that I find a lot more effective. Our emotions stem from our perspectives;
if we reframe our perspective even just a fraction, our emotions will change.

Positive Reframing

This is a very simple type of reframing. It's probably the most common type and most people can do it in a lot of situations, often without realizing. It involves taking something you used to view as negative and focusing on positive things instead.

Positive reframing could also include considering a negative situation and asking yourself how you can look at this negative situation in a more positive way. This is the same as 'looking on the bright side' or 'looking for silver linings'. It usually involves you proactively seeking out another perspective or view to experience a situation from.

Think back to the last time you felt you weren't as resilient as you wanted to be. Were there any positives to come out of the situation? You might feel better about that situation now because your view of it has changed naturally. Unfortunately, this type of reframing doesn't work in all instances, because sometimes the negative perspective persists and continues to be a potential source for negative emotions. Due to negativity bias and primary bias (see box, page 51), you're more likely to give more weight to the original negative perspective. If you're thinking about a past occasion where you weren't as resilient as you wanted to be, you might be able to see it differently and create a more positive view, but may still focus on the fact that you weren't as resilient as you wanted to be.

These biases could certainly account for why it's harder to think of yourself as resilient when there's already a competing pre-existing belief that you're not resilient. If you believe you're not resilient, it's potentially going to be harder to believe anything else. For this reason, it's easier to dismantle that belief rather than trying to replace it with another.

Other Person Reframing

This is another simple form of reframing, which involves seeing an event or situation from someone else's point of view.

When we interpret something, it's easy to be stuck within that interpretation as if that's the only interpretation we can possibly entertain. An easy way to get unstuck is to see it from the point of view of another person. This should immediately dispel the notion that the situation is only viewable from one perspective, the one you're currently entertaining.

There's an idea in psychology called 'functional fixedness'. This is when we're unable to solve problems because we are affected by self-imposed restrictions in our thinking. We presuppose there's only one way to look at a situation, so we feel stuck. This is why certain riddles are hard to solve, because they encourage us to think about the problem in a certain way – a way that makes solving the riddle harder.

Lateral thinking or thinking outside of the box is one way of breaking free from this self-imposed restriction. Thinking there can only be one perspective is an example of functional fixedness. Acknowledging that different people might see an event or situation differently from you, even if it's only slightly differently, is one way of breaking free.

If you're in a situation where you're not exhibiting as much resilience as you would like, think of another person and ask yourself, how might they find a way of being more resilient in this scenario? What would they focus on?

Other Person Reframing & Grief

Other person reframing is particularly useful when helping someone through the grieving process. Emotional pain is often one of the most challenging aspects of grief. A lot of people who go through this process think they *should* be feeling painful emotions. An effective question to ask someone who seems stuck in the pain of the grief is, 'How do you think the person you're grieving would want you to feel?' Most people instantly realize that their loved one would obviously not want them to feel pain while thinking about them. Before this question is asked, that person's resilience to their understandably difficult pain could be non-existent. Afterwards, their resilience usually immediately increases.

Grief can also be reframed by considering how cultures around the world mourn the death of their loved ones differently. In the Balinese culture, for example, it's much more common for the emphasis to be placed upon celebrating their loved one's life, rather than mourning their death.

KIKI: REFRAMING A CHALLENGE AS AN OPPORTUNITY

The Japanese word for 'crisis' – *kiki* – is the same as the word for 'opportunity', and is made up of two characters, 'danger' and 'opportunity'. Discovering this helped me see that a reframing mechanic has been built into the Japanese language. It can be useful to remember this example at challenging times. If we see something as a problem, we understandably may want someone to come and take it away from us or resolve it for us. But if we see it as an opportunity, we probably won't want someone to take it away. We're more likely to engage with it and know it's going to help us develop.

Best Perspective Reframing

The types of reframing we've looked at so far have been similar in terms of their structure, which is the equivalent of looking at one part of a picture and then telling yourself to look at another part of the picture or a different picture altogether. The disadvantage to these types of reframe is that the first picture still exists, so negative emotions can ensue.

A better type of reframing is one that helps you see that original picture in a different way. An example of this is what I call 'best perspective reframing'. It's more complicated than the other types of reframing, but whereas those won't work in every situation, this one can.

If we're feeling negative, there's a good chance we could feel better by looking at reality in a different way. The data isn't going to change, but our perspective on the data can. We can use that same data to create a different story or narrative. At all times, our brains have the perpetual task of supplying only the best narrative they can based on the data provided. If we're not aware of this, we may naturally assume our current view is the best view, without questioning this. There are three areas or categories of 'best' we can consider checking.

The Three Categories of Best

We can check to see if a current story or narrative is the best narrative by looking at it in three different ways:

Category 1: Is My Narrative the Most Realistic Option?

We often place too high an expectation on ourselves or on other people or on life. Rather than lowering those expectations to a level that's more realistic, we rigidly hold on to them and get upset when they're not met. Often our perspectives are actually demands. It's certainly not the most realistic perspective to maintain that such and such must happen, especially when it's currently not happening.

Category 2: Is My Narrative the Most Sensible Option?

Ask ourself if your story is sensible or if it is based on assumptions, flawed logic or contradictions. A lot of negative emotions are based on assumptions. Not all assumptions will turn out to be false but we shouldn't treat an assumption as if it's evidence-based. Our brains are governed by logic but it's sometimes difficult to notice when logic is flawed. We make connections between things but sometimes those connections don't exist outside of our creation of them. In other words, we connect dots that aren't there. Sometimes our perspectives contradict what's out there in reality but we don't notice because we're looking elsewhere.

Category 3: Is My Narrative the Most Helpful & Empowering Option?

When undesirable events happen, an important aspect of our perspective is our starting point or stance. We can entertain different general types of stances, outlined below.

- Adopting a victim stance involves you feeling powerless. You want reality to be different but you think you lack the agency to affect change. You feel like you don't have adequate resilience to cope with the situation.
- A survivor stance is more empowering. You acknowledge you've got resilience so you're more likely to withstand or bounce back. You recognize you do have agency and try to use that agency in the best way to make the most of the situation.
- A warrior stance is the most empowering. You acknowledge you are now stronger because of the undesirable event, and you have more resilience and agency. You will use this

agency in the best way possible to make the most of the situation for yourself or even others in similar situations.

Using the Categories of Best

There's a hierarchy to the three categories of best. The potential helpfulness of a story outweighs its apparent realisticness or how sensible (logical) it is. If we're not letting go of a story that we know isn't the best, what's helpful about it? How is this perspective serving you better than all the other infinite possibilities?

Highlighting precisely how you think the current perspective is helping you can make certain unhelpful aspects apparent and allow you to look at it in a more objective way. This is sometimes challenging to achieve because of the subconscious nature of emotions. The emotion is underpinned by subconscious reasoning, so we would benefit from making that subconscious reasoning conscious.

I often use the example of anger to illustrate this, because anger is an emotion that a lot of people have difficulty letting go of. It can be prompted by someone breaking one of your moral codes or by you perceiving some sort of crime. To your subconscious, anger is the best way to address these transgressions, but in reality it can often make the situation worse. Someone might do something you don't like and you could respond with anger. That might resolve the situation and encourage the person to stop, but it could go the other way too – that person could respond to your anger with anger of their own. So rather than anger being the best way to resolve a situation, your anger might make the situation worse. It might not be helpful.

Not being able to let go after feeling angry also involves flawed logic. Someone might not want to let go of their anger because they think it would be the same as condoning the offending behaviour or letting it go unaddressed. But you don't have to be angry to address bad behaviour. Also, if your anger is a result of a crime being committed, feeling angry means you're punishing yourself for someone else's crime, which is more flawed logic. Feeling angry is not sensible.

Why Best Perspective Reframing Works

It might seem challenging to let go of a certain narrative or story, but when we see the dots we're connecting, we may find it easier. This directly relates to an important aspect of resilience, bouncing back. We're not going to bounce back if we're holding on to a negative emotion.

Best perspective reframing is different to positive reframing and other person reframing because it is simply questioning whether our view of an event or situation really is the best perspective or not. We don't have to generate another view of the situation when we reframe in this way. We just need to highlight any ways in which our view might not be the best perspective. Our narrative can then be dropped, and a better version of it should automatically emerge and overwrite the previous one. This removes the possibility of having two competing views, which is the disadvantage of the other types of reframing. Instead of holding on to competing views, we will hold on only to the one that makes most sense.

A Four-step Reframing Process

With a structured approach, we can consciously influence the usually subconscious narratives that we generate using best perspective reframing. We can resolve negative emotions or feelings and consciously influence our emotions by following a simple four-step plan.

The stages of this four-step plan are explained below. It can be helpful to think about these using the ACE framework (see page 50), in which A is the activating event, C is the concept (or narrative), and E is the emotion.

1. **Identify the emotion.** Do this so you're not lost in the details of the story, which is very easily done. In terms of the ACE framework, what's the E?
2. **Acknowledge that the emotion is perspective-driven, not event-driven.** The event isn't prompting our emotion; our interpretation of the event is. This is a reminder that our emotions aren't directly based on events, but are directly

based on our perspective of the event. The E isn't based on the A; it's based on the C.

3. **Ask, what's the perspective?** What's the A? What are the facts of the situation? Then, what's the C? What's your interpretation of what happened? Remind yourself it's just one perspective out of many. It's supposed to the best one. We can validate the part of us that believes that our particular interpretation is the best because it believes it for a good reason. Once we have done that, we can move onto the final step.
4. **Confirm whether that perspective actually is the best story by looking at the three different categories of best.** Is your interpretation the most realistic, the most sensible and logical, and the most helpful and empowering? If it's not, it can be automatically dropped. If we find it too difficult to drop it, we can ask ourselves, why are we holding on to it? Why is this perspective better than the other infinite possible perspectives.

If we feel unable to drop a particular perspective, it might be because our subconscious thinks that holding on to it is more helpful than dropping it – part of us still believes it is the best. We think if we let go of it, we will be in a worse position. If that's the case, we could ask ourselves how? How are we going to be in a worse position? We can acknowledge that our bad feeling isn't preventing that bad thing from happening. We're more likely to prevent the bad thing from happening if we're not feeling negatively because we'll be able to focus on the situation rather than being distracted by any negative feelings that come up.

Our stories should be only the best stories – the most realistic, the most sensible and the most helpful and empowering. Entertaining a story that's not the best is like drinking poison. Even if there's a small amount of poison in a drink, having *any* of that drink is a bad idea. Feeling the negative emotion is your body's reaction to the poison. This reframing process identifies that the drink has poison in it and we can discard it. Our thoughts and stories are not reality; they are a way of us making sense of reality in the most realistic, sensible, useful and empowering way.

Turnaround Time

Everybody is already using a method to reframe events, but most peoples' versions are unconscious, indirect, unstructured and/or unintentional. Four-step best perspective reframing is conscious, direct, structured and intentional. Once we start practising it, we can drastically reduce the time it takes for us to feel better after feeling negatively.

In reframing terms, turnaround time is the time it takes to look at an event from a better perspective, either by generating a new one or dismantling the old one. Without a conscious or structured process, the turnaround time depends on us indirectly reframing or waiting for someone else to reframe for us. If we're feeling negatively about something, the quicker we reframe the event, the shorter the turnaround time will be.

We can use reframing to bolster our ability to withstand challenging events. If we didn't withstand these as well as we would have liked, we can use it to shorten the turnaround time and bounce back to a more normal state. Holding on to the emotion is the main thing preventing us from bouncing back quicker.

Some people say that time is a healer; you must just wait and let time pass and you will feel better. This is not strictly true. Time isn't a healer directly – the key ingredient in healing is generating a better story and it sometimes takes time to do that.

Our stories are subconscious or unconscious. We may have already subconsciously told ourselves something based on the data as we initially perceived it and because of this, reality appears to be a certain way. We often believe this initial perspective is the only way reality can be. Sometimes our perspective is the best perspective because it's the only perspective now, but in fact it's just one out of many options. Even though our initial stories are subconscious, we can always challenge the original story or generate another one consciously.

One way to significantly shorten the turnaround time is to consciously challenge it. At first, you may be too busy being affected by the negative event to be in the right frame of mind to even think about challenging your narrative, so gaining this level of awareness or mindfulness may take practice. If you don't have the presence of mind to think about your narrative while you're experiencing the event, doing so soon after would be beneficial, because that will prompt a quicker turnaround or bounce-back time.

Key Takeaways

- We can change how resilient we feel by changing our perspective on events using reframing techniques.
- We can check if our current narrative is the best narrative using the three categories of best: is it the most realistic, the most sensible, and the most helpful?
- Four-step best perspective reframing helps us dismantle our current perspective and confidently let go of negative emotions that prevent us from bouncing back.
- Turnaround time is the time it takes us to see an event from a different perspective and feel better, more helpful emotions that can help us withstand situations.

CHAPTER FOUR

Emotions

How we feel is possibly the biggest obstacle to resilience. Our resilience is directly tied to our negative emotions: we can't withstand some events because we're trying to avoid negative emotions; and we don't bounce back quickly because we're holding on to negative emotions. Reframing shows how easily emotions can be replaced or treated as if they are not there, so why do negative emotions exist? If we understood our emotions better, we would more easily manage them and lead more fulfilling and happier lives while being constantly resilient. Once negative emotions are broken down, we'll see why they may be the biggest obstacle to resilience.

The Logic Behind Negative Emotions

It would be difficult to describe emotions comprehensively without talking about logic. It's a common misconception that people are either logical or emotional, when in fact everybody is both all the time. Our emotions are based on our beliefs and our beliefs are based on logic. Therefore, our emotions are based on logic.

There's a definite and knowable logical reason for feeling every emotion we feel. If we don't know the reason immediately, we can explore and identify it. If the current emotion isn't the most sensible emotion to feel in a particular situation, we would instead feel another emotion that better fits the situation.

All our negative emotions have themes. By negative emotions, I mean the eight pairs of healthy and unhealthy emotions identified in Chapter 2 (see pages 46–7). You feel an emotion because you're telling yourself a specific type of story underpinned with a certain logic. If you told yourself a different story, you would feel a different emotion. Here are the stories, or themes, for each pair of negative emotions:

- The theme for depression and sadness is failure or loss. To feel depressed or sad, we're telling ourselves a story with a sense of failure or loss at its core.
- Anxiety and concern/worry follows a perception of threat.
- Anger and frustration stems from a belief that someone has broken at least one of our moral codes.

- The theme for hurt and disappointment is that someone close to us has treated us unfairly or an expectation has not been met.
- The theme for shame and regret is a perception of our conduct being substandard. There's often overlap with guilt and shame, so stories often contain both.
- Guilt and remorse emerge when we think we have done something we shouldn't have or haven't done something we should.
- People often use the word 'jealous' when they probably mean 'envious'. The theme for envy is that someone has something that we want but don't have, whereas jealousy emerges when we believe that someone or something is threatening an important relationship we have. There's often overlap between these two emotions. We could be jealous of an attractive colleague of our partner because we think they're a potential threat to the relationship, and we could also be envious of their physical features.

Why Do Negative Emotions Exist?

Our levels of resilience are tied to our emotions. We often experience an apparent lack of resilience because we think showing resilience will lead to a negative outcome, and imagining that outcome leads to a negative emotion. A better understanding of why we have negative emotions will help.

We have subconscious control of our emotions. There are lots of different theories about why negative emotions exist, but the fact that we have subconscious control of our emotions disproves a lot of these theories. We're going to examine two commonly held theories and see how they can be easily disputed. I'll then introduce a third theory that may sound a bit out there, but I have conducted research that scientifically proves it. Our negative emotions are there for a reason, and this chapter will shine a light on what that is.

Theory 1: The Function Theory

This theory says that negative emotions exist because, in certain situations, they are more useful than positive emotions. For example, negative emotions are the best forms of motivation.

A lot of people think negative emotions are deterrents for negative behaviour. The idea is that someone might think about doing something bad, but then have feelings of guilt and shame and so be deterred from doing the bad thing. However, people can think about doing something bad, feel guilt and shame but *still* do that bad thing.

With no apparent exceptions, every positive use of a negative emotion can be shown to have a correlative relationship rather than a causative one. For example, saying anger is useful because it's a form of motivation isn't the whole truth. You can be angry *and* motivated, but that doesn't mean that you *need* to be angry to be motivated. If anger is a good strategy to get what you want in some situations, feeling calm and negotiating with the person is usually a more consistently effective strategy.

The function theory can be generally disproved by considering that when we feel negative emotions, our ability to think clearly is adversely affected. Surely thinking clearly is going to benefit you more than not thinking clearly in any situation?

Thinking negative emotions are useful for reasons like deterring bad behaviour and improving motivation is like not knowing how valuable a bar of gold is and using it as a paperweight. The bar will serve its current purpose and hold the paper down but it's a lot more valuable than that. Negative emotions might be somewhat useful, but we can appreciate them in a different way if we realize their original function.

Theory 2: The Inevitability Theory

According to this theory, having negative emotions is unavoidable. There's no reason to them, they're just there, which means we're going to feel them from time to time.

On the surface, this theory seems true because our negative emotions seem so prevalent, but I think it's truer to say that negative *events* are inevitable. Things are going to happen that we don't like. I don't think it's as true to say that we're bound to feel bad because of those negative events. The fact that we can reframe events generally disproves this. We may have felt negative emotions after an event because of the way we interpreted it, but that interpretation can change with time. And if we had interpreted it in that different way originally, we could have avoided the negative emotion in the first place.

Theory 3: The Baby Theory

This theory suggests that negative emotions in adults are merely a remnant of a (now obsolete) process we used as babies to ensure our needs and desires were met.

I formulated this theory over thirty years ago and suspected its truthfulness back then, because it makes more sense than all the alternative theories out there. Despite trying, I've been unable to disprove it. The theory may be hard to accept for some people, but I have conducted research that provides data to support it.

Let's begin by going all the way back to when we were babies. Ideally, a baby is in a state of comfort, equilibrium or homeostasis (a state of internal balance.) When there's less than ideal nutrition or temperature or if the baby is in pain, a state of disequilibrium or imbalance is triggered. Disequilibrium feels uncomfortable.

As the baby is very fragile and dependent, they can't resolve the issue causing this discomfort themselves and they don't have any other way of communicating. They cry so that someone more able to resolve the situation is alerted. That person tends to the baby, problem solves and makes the necessary adjustments to the internal or external environment to restore equilibrium or balance so the baby feels comfortable again. This function or process is used to ensure the baby's needs are met as quickly as possible. The baby notices a connection between bad feelings and equilibrium restoration.

When the baby starts to have desires as well as needs, and perceives obstructions to those desires, they induce a negative feeling and then express it to get their desires met in the same way they used it to get their needs met. They make themselves feel bad and start crying so that an adult gives them what they want, in the same way they used to feel bad and cry so that an adult gave them what they needed. This tactic works more times than not, so an association is made between feeling bad and getting what they want.

When we grow up, we're not taught about this automatic and universal process and so other theories take precedence in terms of explaining why negative emotions exist. Bad sensations are helpful – for example, pain is a signal that we are being harmed. But negative emotions are not helpful, because we're still running a now-obsolete problem-solving mechanic that we used to get our desires met as babies.

Now that we are older, we can meet our desires ourselves, verbally ask for assistance or realize that not all of our desires will be met and that's okay.

This theory is a lot to take in when it's first shared. I usually ask the person I'm sharing it with to not take my word for it, and instead urge them to actively try to think of exceptions. A sound theory is one that has not been disproved, so I ask them if they can disprove it. I point out that the theory can be potentially disproved if they can think of a time when they felt bad and there wasn't at least one thing about the situation they wanted changed. In the thirty-plus years since formulating this theory, I have yet to come across any examples of this.

I described negativity bias in Chapter 2 (see box, page 51). This theory explains why we give more weight to perceived negatives than we do to perceived positives. Negative emotions are tied to problems. We don't need to tend to positive things in the same way, because there isn't an apparent problem to be solved.

A lot of people who subscribe to the function theory say that emotional pain is a useful signal to let us know when things aren't right, just like physical pain is a useful signal to let us know when our bodies are being harmed. But there's a big difference between physical pain and emotional pain. Physical pain is caused by a harmful intrusion of some kind. Emotional pain is caused by how we're interpreting something. So, if negative emotions are signals, they're only signals that we've interpreted something in a certain way.

Objections to the Baby Theory

Not everybody accepts the Baby Theory when they first hear it, and I have heard a few recurring objections over the last three decades:

Why Is This Theory Not Known Already?

The first general objection I heard was, if this is true, why aren't more people already seeing it? The answer is we may not be seeing it as easily because we're taught something else about why negative emotions exist, or we adopt other reasons and then we become biased towards to those things – primary bias (see box, page 51). There may be similar theories that focus solely on babies, which fail to acknowledge that the automatic mechanism of making ourselves feel bad in order to get our desires met is still running in adults. If we only did this process as babies, when did we stop doing it?

What About When We Feel Bad About Nothing?

I think it's highly unlikely that we can feel bad about nothing. It's much more likely that every time we feel bad, there's always a trigger, but sometimes that trigger will be outside of our awareness. In other words, there is something that we don't like but we don't consciously know what it is. Exploration could bring the problem into awareness. If we really don't know what it is, we can focus on the bad emotion and that could highlight it. As our bad emotions all have themes (see pages 72–3), identifying the appropriate theme could highlight the subconscious story that's prompting the emotion.

One Size Can't Fit All.

Some people have expressed doubt at one theory being applicable to everybody. Different brains work differently, they say, so how can one theory possibly fit them all? What about people who are neurodivergent, so have conditions such as ADHD or autism? What about people with an imbalance of some kind, whether it's hormonal or chemical? What about someone who's clinically depressed?

I think this theory covers these conditions too. If you have a hormonal or chemical imbalance, you're still using the same process, but the emotional response is more magnified. You may perceive more triggers because of the imbalance. Those triggers may prompt more intense feelings and those feelings might last longer, but the feelings stem from the same biological process.

Adults Feel Bad About Different Things to Babies. We're Taught to Self-soothe & Don't Always Talk to Someone When We're Feeling Bad.

Another argument is that negative emotions can't be about securing a change to satisfy unmet needs or desires, because we often feel negative emotions yet we don't communicate these to other people. That is true, but remember this is a subconscious process. The person who's feeling negative doesn't know the ultimate reason for this because they believe their negative feeling is rooted elsewhere. Also, because this is a subconscious process, we can feel negatively about something that has no chance of changing.

It's true that adults don't feel bad about the same things they did as babies, but the general process of generating negative emotions is the same: it's a conditioned response triggered by the perception of a problem of some kind. We're taught to self-soothe in a less than ideal way. We're encouraged to not cry over spilt milk, but we're not encouraged to better understand the negative feeling that prompts the crying. If we spill milk, we may not cry about it, but we can certainly feel bad about it. Being taught to not cry over spilt milk is really teaching us to suppress our emotions, not to better understand them.

How Could It Be Possible to Not Feel Negative Emotions?

People have asked, even if you take the theory onboard, how are you not going to feel negative emotions in extremely negative situations? How are you not going to feel bad when someone dies? The simple answer is most people are going to feel bad in those events because we feel bad when something happens that we don't like.

The fact that we can feel almost unbearably painful emotions at some events but mildly uncomfortable emotions at other times supports the theory and adds detail. There's a connection between the intensity and duration of the feeling relative to the significance of the thing. There is a clear linear relationship. If we want something small changed, we might make ourselves feel a little uncomfortable and if the change isn't forthcoming, we'll move on. If we want a big change, we're going to make ourselves feel extremely uncomfortable. We will subconsciously do everything in our power to get that change and that unfortunately means making yourself feel as uncomfortable as possible for as long as possible. That's why grief feels as painful and the bereavement process lasts as long as it does. The general pattern is, the more we want something to be different and it isn't, the worse we make ourselves feel.

Quite a few people who were previously on the fence about the Baby Theory, or disbelieved it, saw the sense in the theory when they considered this linear relationship, because we all have lots of experiences where we had intense emotional reactions to important things and less intense reactions to trivial things.

How We Can Use the Baby Theory

The other theories to explain why negative emotions exist are circumstantial, so may seem to be true to some people some of the time; the Baby Theory seems to apply to everybody, and that makes sense, because we were all babies once. We feel negative emotions only when we want an aspect of our experience to change because it's something that we don't like – even, as mentioned above, things that can't be changed. Expressing a negative sensation or emotion is the only way a baby can prompt change. And all the things that we didn't like as babies *could* be changed.

If this theory is true, negative emotions occur because we subconsciously think they are the best type of intervention to make when we perceive problems. It's a conditioned response, but we can condition a healthier response by acknowledging the situation and looking at other options.

We could interpret the problem differently, so that it's no longer viewed as a problem. It could be a blessing in disguise, an opportunity to learn something important that could benefit us in other ways. If we took that stance, we wouldn't want to make the situation disappear; instead we would be more likely to engage and learn from it. That would be an example of reframing the story or narrative about the event.

You could also change your view by acknowledging that negative emotions aren't the best type of intervention. In some ways, they're the worst intervention, because of their impact on our ability to think clearly and problem solve.

Key Takeaways

- Our resilience is tied to our negative emotions, so managing our emotions is a good way to manage our resilience.
- We have negative emotions only because we needed them as babies to prompt someone to resolve unmet needs (and later desires), and this process has continued into adulthood.
- Understanding why we have negative emotions allows us to respond differently to problems.

CHAPTER FIVE

Splitting the Emotional Atom

The previous chapter highlighted a sensible theory that explains why negative emotions still exist in adults. This chapter will dissect negative emotions. It will explain what's happening at the moment you feel negatively by breaking down the process into the constituent parts. It will also share lots of helpful analogies that will help deepen your understanding of how our emotions work. Our emotional responses are deeply embedded conditioned responses. Once we can understand these conditioned responses, we will be better able to decondition them and start to recondition a healthier and more helpful response.

Stages of Emotional Development

Many psychologists who have studied child development have identified stages of emotional development we experience, but those stages don't take the Baby Theory (see page 76) into account. Looking at our emotions through a microscope suggests there are different stages of emotional development and important aspects to those stages that have yet to be identified.

Stage One: The Newborn Baby (0–3 Months)

At this stage there are only positive sensations and negative sensations. Positive sensations accompany ideal conditions; the baby is feeling comfortable or is in a state of homeostasis or equilibrium or balance, because all of their needs are being met. Their nutrition level and temperature are within ideal ranges and they're not in any pain from an internal or external source. They only feel negative sensations when their needs are not being met and their senses reflect a less than ideal internal environment due to nutrition levels, or a less than ideal external environment due to temperature, or if they're in pain. This triggers a state of disequilibrium, imbalance or discomfort.

The newborn communicates this discomfort by crying, and these expressions are usually met with swift action. A caregiver tends to the baby, identifies the need that's not being met and meets it. This leads to equilibrium restoration and feelings of comfort.

The baby continues to use this process to ensure their needs are met as quickly as possible. Through simple association, the newborn makes a connection between feeling discomfort, intervention from a caregiver and then feeling comfort again. This connection is reinforced countless times a day and becomes embedded in our subconscious in a way that will become difficult to separate.

Stage Two: The Older Baby (3–18 Months)

Something very interesting happens in this stage: we start convincing ourselves of four illusions that we are still falling for as adults: the illusion of better, the illusion of need, the illusion of discomfort and the illusion of control.

We're no longer satisfied with just equilibrium or comfort; we want entertainment and pleasure and we start to have desires. This is the basis of the first illusion, the illusion of better – we distinguish between two things and make a judgement based on that distinction. This prompts the second illusion, the illusion of need; we don't just see this so-called better thing and want it, we think we *need* it.

The senses reflect conditions that lead to disequilibrium when there's an unmet need in the first stage as a newborn, and we express this discomfort by crying in order to alert someone and hopefully enact a change. That process changes in this second stage, because there's an important difference between an unmet need and an unmet desire. There's a naturally occurring bad sensation when there's an unmet need. There aren't any naturally occurring bad sensations when there's an unmet desire, so we must create one by self-inducing discomfort.

This is the third illusion and the birth of negative emotions: the illusion of discomfort. With these bad emotions, we trick ourselves into thinking we're in a potentially life-threatening situation. We create a negative emotion by convincing ourselves that we are experiencing a negative sensation, that we are hungry, too hot, too cold or in pain, and trick ourselves into thinking the negative sensation has been forced upon us as opposed to being self-induced. We make this illusion so convincing that we can't distinguish between a negative emotion and a real negative sensation. As far as we're concerned, there's an unmet need that requires urgent attention. We get urgent attention more times than not, so the effectiveness of this plan is reinforced countless times a day. The constant reinforcement leads to the final illusion, the illusion of control. We think we can control our environment by how we feel because our negative feelings usually prompt intervention.

At this stage, we have positive sensations when our needs are met and negative sensations when they're not. We now also have positive emotions when our desires are met and negative emotions when they're not. All of the illusions contained within the negative emotions seem intertwined and simultaneous.

Exposing the Illusion

This chapter is called 'splitting the emotional atom'. By this, I mean breaking down the emotion to its smallest components. We can appreciate what is happening with more detail when we have a better understanding of all the parts and how they connect to or interact with one another.

The different parts of the negative emotion can be mapped to the different illusions described above. All four illusions must be active for the negative emotion to exist, so seeing through any of them will end the negative feeling.

The Illusion of Better

Or, the grass is greener. How many times have you thought something was going to be better and it wasn't? This is slightly different to the illusion of better referred to in Chapter 1 (see page 29). In that earlier instance, the illusion of better hinged on us not being aware of relevant choices. This illusion of better hinges on an arbitrary judgement of something. That thing isn't better, it's just different.

The Illusion of Need

How many times do people use the word 'need' when they really mean 'want'? When I say 'need', I mean if this thing is consistently obstructed, we are going to die so under that criterion, our needs are sustenance, sleep, oxygen and shelter depending on what part of the planet we're on and the time of year. Everything else are desires and some of those desires are labelled by some as psychological or emotional needs.

The Illusion of Discomfort

All emotions are internally generated. Happiness comes from within, so the same applies to unhappiness. Specific emotions are dictated by current experience; they stem from the specific way we interpret events.

The Illusion of Control

Every time we feel negative emotions, we do so because our subconscious thinks that negative emotion is going to lead to a change in reality. I've had some interesting conversations about this general illusion of control in adults. People usually regard control as absolute authority, but we don't have absolute authority over anything; instead we have choices, and some of those choices are enacted. People are often disturbed when their illusion of control has been shattered because certain surefire choices are obstructed. The definition of control is 'influence'. If we acknowledged that, we would probably exercise this influence better, because we would be more flexible, relaxed and resourceful.

Analogies to Start Deconditioning

Now that we've identified the general theory of why we experience negative emotions and exposed the illusions we've been falling for pretty much our whole lives, we can start to decondition our very entrenched conditioned response.

I'll describe six analogies that will help deepen our understanding of how our emotions work. I created most of these, but others were conceived by other people after accepting the Baby Theory. All four illusions (of better, need, discomfort and control) are interwoven in most of the analogies, but some analogies focus mainly on just one or two of the illusions. After reading the analogies below, it might be beneficial to have a go at creating your own. Ask yourself, how could I say this in a different way? After you've sat with the theory for a while, you might find that other analogies naturally come to mind. Creating your own analogies could significantly expedite the deconditioning process.

Analogy 1: The Magician's Trick

Would you fall for a magician's trick if you knew how it worked? You might still appreciate the craft and remember the 'Wow' feeling you experienced when you first saw the trick, but would you be as impressed after the method has been exposed?

With the new understanding of how negative emotions work thanks to the Baby Theory, we can appreciate the emotional pain we feel is self-induced rather than imposed upon us. Emotional pain is merely us creating a feeling of discomfort. If we hadn't been conditioned by this illusion of discomfort when we were babies, we may not have created negative emotions that led us to act in order to motivate another person to help us in our time of 'urgent need'. As an adult you know this process of creating negative emotions is an illusion, and you now have a better understanding of how and why the illusion works.

The point of this analogy is to make clear that if we know how a trick works, it shouldn't be so easy to succumb to it. But even though we can learn our negative emotions are basically illusory, that doesn't necessarily mean we're not going to fall for this illusion any more. The reason for this is that there's a part of our brain that will try to ensure we do. This is the part that is committed to doing what it can to ensure our desires are met, unless we make a conscious effort to condition another response, which is the focus of the next analogy.

Analogy 2: Hiroo Onoda

After the Second World War ended in 1945, some squads of Japanese soldiers continued fighting because they didn't know the war was over. A soldier named Hiroo Onoda, based on a remote island in the Philippines, led one of these squads. Various methods were used to spread the word of Japan's surrender, but the soldiers thought it was merely the enemy trying to trick them into falsely surrendering. The soldiers didn't accept that Japan had lost. They were told to never surrender and never back down, so they continued protecting the land they were commanded to protect.

One by one the soldiers died until only Hiroo survived, and he continued to fight. After countless attempts to convey the message of Japan's defeat to him had failed, someone found him and asked him what it would take for him to believe the war was over. Hiroo said he would believe the news only if his commanding officer told him, as it was he who had commanded him to never surrender. His commanding officer, who was still alive, was tracked down. He personally delivered the message and Hiroo finally stood down. He had continued fighting for twenty-nine years after the war had ended.

I couldn't comprehend that level of dedication when I first heard this story. I then realized that it can be compared to the our brain's unwavering commitment to making ourselves feel bad in order to try to fix something we think is broken. This analogy makes it clear that telling ourselves that this process no longer works is not enough; the instruction must come from an authoritative source, or our subconscious is not going to believe it and make the necessary changes. Without an instruction from an authoritative source, that part of our brain will continue doing what it was designed to do because it used to be very effective.

Analogy 3: Wrestling

This analogy highlights the illusions of discomfort and control. When I was growing up, I watched wrestling on television most Saturday afternoons. I remember thinking it was a real sport until I learnt that all the matches were choreographed. Once I discovered this type of wrestling was staged, it was impossible for me to see it in any other way, to the point of wondering how I hadn't realized it sooner. Learning the truth behind our negative emotions should be similar.

Imagine you are a wrestling promoter. You spend one million pounds a year putting on a wrestling show because you know you'll make four million pounds in ticket sales. Imagine if the ticket sales went right down to zero for the next few years – would you continue to spend a million pounds?

We are doing something with our emotions that we clearly wouldn't do with our money. Having a negative emotion and expecting a certain outcome, and then not getting that outcome but continuing to have negative emotions is like spending money putting on a wrestling show knowing that nobody's going to show up. Not only are you not going to get the result you want (make four million pounds), you're going to be worse off because you're definitely going to be one million pounds down.

Continuing to feel bad solely because it used to be an effective strategy doesn't make sense, considering it hasn't been an effective strategy for a while. Our negative feelings used to be helpful when we were babies, but now they just compound problems. They make it harder to resolve situations because now we have to deal with our bad feelings as well as trying to resolve the original problem.

Analogy 4: Installing Updates

Learning about the Baby Theory but then retaining the same attitude towards negative emotions is like not updating the operating system of your brain. You'd be using the very first operating system, rather than the latest release, which will bring with it a whole host of new features designed to create a more enjoyable user experience.

This analogy drives home the idea that the brain is a computer. It's a supercomputer, but a computer nonetheless, and computers use software and run programs. Negative feelings are part of a program that was useful at one stage but is now not only not useful, it is getting in the way. It's feasible to suggest that most if not all of the issues that people face aren't impacting them as much as this program, because this program is getting in the way of us solving issues ourselves. Most problems are immediately identifiable, so you can start to work on them or accept that you can't affect change. Unfortunately, this program is hidden. If it remains hidden, we're not going to get what we want as easily.

Analogy 5: Petrol

Someone I shared the Baby Theory with created this analogy. He said feeling bad about something is like trying to put out a fire by adding petrol. The analogy highlights the idea that adding fuel to a fire is certainly not the best way to extinguish it. If there's an external problem, generating an internal problem isn't the best way to resolve it.

Analogy 6: The Genie Lamp

This is my favourite analogy, and it brings us back to the second stage of our emotional development where the illusions were created. Imagine we have a genie lamp. Every time we think there's an obstacle and we want reality to be different, we wish it to be so and we rub a genie lamp. Rubbing the lamp creates discomfort and it prompts a genie (a caregiver), who can grant all of our wishes immediately. The older we get, the less reliable the genie becomes, because our wishes get more complex and often unable to be granted.

One day the genie moves out, so they're no longer there to grant wishes. The lamp is broken. But we continue rubbing the lamp. For years now, we've continued to give ourselves discomfort, even though our wishes do not get granted. The chances of solving the problem ourselves is greatly diminished because our negative feelings often become the priority: we're too adversely affected by how bad we're feeling to think about the problem in a helpful way.

You could say this broken lamp is also cursed, so this broken, cursed lamp is preventing us from being more resilient. When we rub the lamp, we're saying that we believe we're not capable or resilient enough, so we subconsciously try to summon help in a way that's not going to work.

When we're feeling negative emotions and we've tried other things to resolve the feeling but those things haven't worked, we could ask ourselves, what wish am I hoping for that's not being granted? Asking and answering this question could give us clarity about what problem we're 'trying' to solve.

Reminding ourselves each time that we are making ourselves uncomfortable to attain this wish will make the idea of rubbing a lamp seem increasingly absurd.

This analogy hopefully makes clear that we don't feel negative emotions because something is broken; instead we feel negative emotions when we try to subconsciously summon a 'magical' force to fix it for us because we unconsciously believe we can't fix it ourselves. Continued use of this lamp facilitates the erosion of resilience.

Over the years, the Serenity Prayer which I mentioned in Chapter 2 (see page 44) has been amended by some people, usually by changing the wording slightly and adding a line or two. Below is my contribution, considering the Baby Theory and analogy of the genie lamp:

> 'Grant me the serenity to accept the things I can't change, the courage to change the things I can and the wisdom to know the difference.
> If I feel any negative emotions, there's something I'm not accepting, and I still want something changed and am trying to change it in a way that's not going to work. Grant me insight to identify whether I need to be more serene, more courageous or wiser.'

Key Takeaways

- Four illusions are created in the second stage of our emotional development: the illusion of better, the illusion of need, the illusion of discomfort and the illusion of control.
- Analogies can help our subconscious realize that negative emotions are merely remnants of a once useful but now obsolete process.
- Creating new analogies could help decondition our response to negative emotions and recondition a healthier and more helpful response more quickly.

CHAPTER SIX

The Growth Mindset

Our emotions determine how resilient we feel, and our emotions are tied to our mindsets, narratives and thoughts. Therefore, a change in mindset can foster resilience. This chapter will describe the growth mindset and the generally very positive default nature of the brain. I'll introduce an idea called the protection paradox, which explains how often our efforts to defend ourselves against perceived threats can create those threats. We stopped being resilient to protect ourselves from something but reduced resilience is now causing issues. Fortunately, changing our behaviour should be easy.

Fixed Versus Growth Mindsets

You've probably heard of the term 'growth mindset'. The concept behind the theory was first developed in the 1980s by psychologist Dr Carol Dweck, who observed something interesting while she was carrying out studies of children. She developed a hypothesis and carried out experiments to test it.

In her experiments, Dr Dweck split children into two groups. She gave the two groups the same set of tests that escalated in difficulty. She told group A they were smart, and group B that they tried hard. The results of the first and simplest test were weighted in favour of group A and they outperformed the other group.

But, when the tests started to increase in complexity, group B started to consistently outperform group A. Dr Dweck felt this was due to group A withdrawing and giving up when they found the tests more challenging. Group B persevered, which lead to them achieving higher scores. They bounced back from disappointing results better than the children in group A. They naturally exhibited more resilience based on what they believed about themselves because of what they had been told – that they tried hard. Thousands of young students were included in these tests and the results were consistent.

Dr Dweck applied two names to these groups: group A had a 'fixed mindset', while group B had a 'growth mindset'. The children in both groups held different ideas about their ability and intelligence which greatly influenced their performance.

When the term 'growth mindset' was coined, Dr Dweck also introduced the idea of a 'false growth mindset'. This was to avoid her ideas being misrepresented. We can see an example of this if we consider the effort aspect of the growth mindset. Effort impacts our abilities and results, but making a certain amount of effort alone doesn't necessarily lead to healthy change, because the wrong type of effort could lead to burnout. The growth mindset principles are maximized when used with other considerations such as accurate perception and feedback.[4]

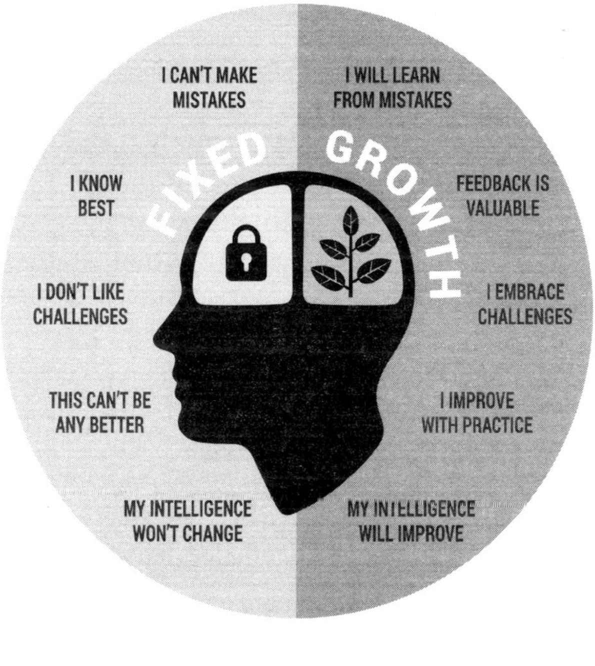

Figure 2. Fixed and growth mindset attributes

The Growth Mindset & Resilience

We are all born with a growth mindset. When we're learning to walk, we fall countless times but that doesn't put us off; we continue trying. The early growth mindset is demonstrated in lots of ways when we're younger. We have a growth mindset until we tell ourselves to stop, leaving room for a fixed mindset to take its place. This conversion usually happens because we received feedback that was negative in some way. Rather than risk receiving further negative feedback, we stop the behaviour that prompted it.

Resilience is the same thing. We are born with impenetrable resilience until we start being more social, and then because of negative feedback, we tell ourselves to stop. Fortunately, the choice to stop can be reversed by making conscious effort. Once you make a certain amount of conscious effort, the new behaviour will become a habit.

As resilience may be inextricably linked to a growth mindset, one way to achieve more resilience is to adopt a growth mindset.

The Growth Mindset & Achievement

To recap, the fixed mindset is the belief that intelligence and ability is static. It leads to a desire to look smart or talented and a tendency to:

- avoid challenges
- get defensive over obstacles
- see effort as pointless

- ignore negative feedback
- feel threatened by others' success

Hence you are less likely to achieve your full potential.

The growth mindset is the belief that intelligence and ability is dynamic and can be developed. It leads to a desire to learn and a tendency to:

- embrace challenges
- persist despite obstacles
- see effort as the path to mastery
- learn from criticism
- find lessons and inspiration from others

Thus you can more easily reach higher levels of achievement.

CHANGE YOUR MINDSET IN FOUR STEPS

One of the misconceptions of a growth mindset is you either have one or you don't. I believe there's a continuum, with a fixed mindset at one extreme and a growth mindset at the other. We occupy different parts of this continuum depending on our activity or mood. If we generally identify with the fixed mindset qualities, such as avoiding challenges and seeing effort as pointless, we may be spending more time on the fixed mindset side of the scale. There are ways of changing this so that you spend more time on the growth mindset side.

Step 1: Acknowledge the continuum and where you are on it.
You may not embrace ***every*** challenge you encounter but you may embrace ***most*** challenges. You may persist despite certain obstacles but withdraw because of others. You may be receptive to some people providing criticism but not others. You might consider some things worth the effort, but not other things.

Step 2: Notice the triggers of a fixed mindset.
Consider when you are more likely to be fixed-mindset orientated. Is it when you're challenged? When there are perceived obstacles? When you think about effort? When you're criticized? When others succeed?

You may find yourself being triggered by certain people rather than certain events. What's different about these people? *Notice the reason or source of the trigger.*

Step 3: Give the triggered part of yourself a persona.
This is so you can separate the triggered part of yourself from the main part of you and interact with it. It can be a past version of yourself, or an alter ego of some kind.

Step 4: Practise remaining in a growth mindset, despite the presence of a trigger, by imagining dialogues with this persona.
These could include supportive inquiries, such as: 'What in particular are you finding challenging about this situation?', and 'Is this a fear-based response? What is the source of the fear?'; or encouragement: 'The more we practice being focused and intentional, the quicker this state will be become natural.' Explore any resistance. Once you have identified what is holding you back, it should be easier to proceed.

The Inhibitory Nature of the Brain

Changing our behaviour should be easy. If it's not, we've probably been traumatized by a past event which has resulted in our brain now being wired differently. But we can rewire it.

We are all born with resilience, along with other innate behaviours. Imagine there's a part of the brain that acts like a fuse box for behaviours that are initially switched on. These include having a growth mindset, resilience, self-love, self-worth, creativity, a sense of curiosity and other traits.

We then have experiences, some of them negative, so we switch these behaviours off, and the fuses become inactive. That means the brain is naturally *disinhibited* – we can do anything we want, unless we think there's a compelling reason not to. In those moments, we consciously or subconsciously choose to *inhibit*.

Making a change of any kind is usually easy. If we're at A and we want to reach B, we should be able to make that journey easily. If the journey isn't an easy process, we've probably been negatively affected by a past event and our brains are now wired differently. We approach B but stop ourselves because of a perceived danger.

Some thoughts, feelings and behaviours are bundled together as neural pathways, which are shortcuts. There are billions of brain cells and a lot of these cells can connect to thousands of others, creating these neural pathways. Some neural pathways are built over time by repetition, but others are created instantly. Imagine walking the same route over some grass again and again; over time, a path will form. Or, you could just steamroll over the grass and create a path instantly. When you learn some things, you have to consciously think about it until a level of proficiency is reached. It then becomes automatic because a neural pathway has been created. Other times, change is more immediate.

Some of the connections we make are created in specific scenarios and then applied globally. For example, you may have been chastized for speaking to someone next to you during assembly in school. You might then have felt acutely embarrassed as you felt the weight of the teacher's negative gaze bearing down on you, as if the whole room was paying attention. This could create a neural pathway of 'don't talk in public' and as a result, you could find it difficult to talk in public for decades to come. You may have been resilient generally, but faltered for a specific reason and then applied that belief to other situations.

Our subconscious mind is quite binary and usually isn't interested in the finer details. That's why a lot of our subconscious strategies are so black and white. Being angry equals protection, so to protect ourselves, we tell ourselves we need to be angry. Being resilient has invited criticism, so to avoid criticism, we tell ourselves we shouldn't be resilient.

Mind Logic & Body Logic

We can distinguish between two different types of logic: *mind* logic and *body* logic. Mind logic is what people usually refer to when they talk about logic. It's the reasoning you can trace out and make explicit. Body logic is a more instinctive 'logic' our bodies respond to because of the reptilian brain. The reptilian brain is the oldest, least developed part of the brain. The newer parts of the brain such as the cortex calculates and reasons, whereas this older part simply reacts.

If you have had a car crash, the next few times you get into a car you may feel extremely apprehensive, because the body logic is determining 'car = crash'. You could use mind logic and try reasoning yourself into a state of relaxation, by thinking about the low odds of being in another crash. You could say there's a 1 per cent chance of being involved in a crash and feel comfortable, because 1 per cent is virtually zero per cent. Body logic, however, is a lot more cautious; it's more likely to see that 1 per cent as 100 per cent, which explains the apprehension. To body logic, even 1 per cent risk is often too much risk – our bodies would much rather play it safe and over-protect us than not protect us enough.

Feelings of fear are very strong. They usually take precedence and are more motivational than any rational thoughts that tell you don't need to be fearful. This is another way we can distinguish between body logic and mind logic: mind logic is the understanding that you only need to feel frightened when you're in danger; body logic is believing you must be in danger because you're feeling frightened.

Mind logic is controlled by the cortex. Body logic is controlled by the autonomic nervous system, which is the part of the brain that tries to ensure that we are always safe.

Some risks are unconscious, but if we can understand the triggers and the proposed risks, we should be in a better position to respond more appropriately.

Trauma & the Protection Paradox

The word 'trauma' is usually used to refer to extreme experiences like abuse or near-death, but it can be prompted by experiencing any event you consider to be negative. If that negative experience rewires your brain and removes the conscious choice of being able to behave in a certain way, there's a strong chance trauma is involved.

Our change from the growth mindset we were born with to a fixed mindset was a maladaptive process prompted by a 'traumatic' event. By maladaptive, I mean we adapted to a situation in a way that wasn't healthy. We saw having a fixed mindset as being preferable, because not doing something was less painful than doing something and getting negative feedback. A common subconscious strategy is to not try something, as this is preferable to trying and failing.

By moving towards a fixed mindset we were supposed to be making a change for the better, but instead we made a change for the worse to protect ourselves from emotional or psychological pain. We stopped being resilient in order to protect ourselves, but that lack of resilience is now causing issues. Unfortunately, we are our own worst enemy – but fortunately, we are our own best ally, too. If we reconciled these forces and understood the underlying motivations better, we would be more resourceful and resilient.

Our attempts to protect ourselves are often counter-productive or self-fulfilling. A self-fulfilling prophecy is when we believe something that isn't true but believing it causes us to act in a certain way, and the result is the thing becoming true. In this context, it can be referred to as the 'protection paradox'.

The protection paradox is when we try to protect ourselves from something that doesn't exist by creating the thing we're trying to protect ourselves from. We're fearful of A, which doesn't exist, but we think it does so we create B, but B is actually A in disguise. For example:

- Someone could start to have doubts about the longevity of a relationship they are in and become overly attached. Their partner could then end the relationship because of this over-attachment.
- Someone could be a people-pleaser because they want people to like them, but they could be disliked for not being genuine.
- Someone could become a perfectionist because they want to perform at a high standard and get good results, but their perfectionism interferes with their performance and results.

If we're aware of this paradox, we're more likely to stop doing what we're doing to protect ourselves, because we realize that it isn't helping and actually making the situation worse.

Key Takeaways

- The fixed mindset and the growth mindset sit at either end of a continuum; we tend to occupy a space closer to one end or the other.
- A growth mindset can help us reach our potential and improve resilience. We were all born with a growth mindset, but some of us switched to a fixed mindset to protect ourselves from painful emotions.
- We can notice when we demonstrate fixed mindset tendencies and change them to growth mindset habits through a four-step process.
- There's mind logic and body logic – understanding what body logic is based on can help us recognize flawed logic and dismantle it.
- Sometimes we create real problems when we try to protect ourselves from imaginary ones – the protection paradox.

CHAPTER SEVEN

Reimagining Anxiety

Sometimes, we may not feel as resilient as we want because we think about doing something difficult that requires us to be resilient, and anxiety comes up. Anxiety is the highest reported mental health issue all over the world, and is often defined as our body's emotional response to a perception of threat. Fortunately, it can usually be relatively easily resolved by learning more about it. This chapter will demystify this emotion so its influence is eliminated or at least reduced.

Dealing with Anxiety

There are many ways we can remove or de-escalate anxiety. I'll outline three different methods below.

Dismantle the Three Pillars of Anxiety

Anxiety and stress have a similar structure. Stress is an emotional response to a perception of pressure; we discussed the four pillars of stress in Chapter 1 (see page 23). Anxiety is an emotional response to a perception of threat, and it has three pillars. All three pillars need to be standing at the same time for you to feel anxiety. Picture a stool to imagine this; kick any one of the legs away and the stool will fall.

1. The first pillar is overestimating the level of threat. In your mind it might be an 8 out of 10 threat, but in reality, it's more like a 2 or 3 out of 10 threat.
2. The second pillar is underestimating your ability to cope with the threat. Let's say you're not overestimating the threat and it is indeed an 8 of 10 threat. If it were an 8 out of 10 threat you believed you could cope with, you wouldn't feel anxiety; you would aim to cope in the best way you could.
3. The third pillar is underestimating the chances of receiving support in the face of the threat. If it were an 8 out of 10 threat that you believed you couldn't cope with but you believed you would receive support, you wouldn't feel anxiety, you would lean into the support.

Removing any one of these pillars will instantly convert the anxiety into the healthier emotion of concern or worry. Sometimes it's unclear which pillar you should work on first, but I usually suggest working on the second, because that's the one we can directly influence. We don't have as much control over the actual level of threat or how much support we receive, but we do have control over our beliefs about how capable we are.

I said earlier that avoidance is a good way to maintain anxiety. This is because you're not allowing yourself to experience the event, which means you will never get the opportunity to realize that a threat may only be a 2 or 3 out of 10 threat rather than the 8 of 10 threat you think it is. If it was an 8 out of 10 threat, you're not allowing yourself to experience the fact that it's an 8 out of 10 threat that you can deal with or receive support for.

Reframe Anxiety

One way to change how you feel about anxiety and change your relationship with it is to change how you view it. Most people view anxiety as something unwanted, something there to spoil fun and to ruin their lives. It's clearly an enemy to them. But a lot of people seem to soften towards their anxiety when they see it more as an overprotective friend, rather than a fun-spoiling enemy. If a friend was trying to overprotect someone, they would possibly first appreciate their friend's effort but make it clear that they feel they don't need protecting. If this was communicated to our anxiety, it might change our view of it and help it protect us only when it is appropriate.

I used to use the overprotective friend analogy to help people reframe their anxiety. I then came across something that seemed more helpful when I saw a television programme called *Dogs Behaving (Very) Badly*,[5] which is about dogs with behavioural issues. In one episode, a dog owner called Rachel had bought an old English sheepdog, Wilson, as a guard dog, because she had been burgled. She felt protected at home but when she took Wilson outside and onto the pavement, he would bark loudly and jump towards any passing traffic, whether it was someone on a scooter or a huge lorry. Rachel contacted the show, and a dog behaviour expert and crew went to investigate.

When the expert saw a demonstration of the dog's behaviour, he asked Rachel why she thought Wilson was acting in this way. Rachel said she thought Wilson was frightened. The expert said he believed Wilson was acting more out of protection than fear. He believed Wilson's behaviour was self-reinforcing in two ways. First, Wilson had good reason to believe that protection was necessary, because he consistently sensed fear from Rachel – he didn't understand she was fearful of his actions, rather than the situation. Secondly, the traffic always went away – Wilson probably believed this was due to how he was behaving, rather than the nature of traffic.

When I saw this television programme, I realized that the dog was precisely mirroring how the subconscious works – the subconscious thinks there's a need for protection, so anxiety is prompted. Also, the subconscious thinks anxiety must be an effective protective response, because we're still alive.

Wilson's behaviour was modified by a process of exposure to the traffic and soothing statements from Rachel. Rachel was encouraged to approach the traffic and remain at a safe distance. Wilson could still see the traffic but wasn't close enough to feel threatened by it. Rachel remained calm and spoke to Wilson in a comforting manner so his calmness was maintained. Rachel then moved towards the traffic in increments until they were able to wait on the pavement without an issue. As Wilson's behaviour mirrored the subconscious, this process mirrors one of the ways that anxiety can be resolved – through exposure, which we'll explore below.

Use a Three-step Process

An effective way of resolving anxiety is to expose yourself to the threat so you can see that it's not as threatening as you think. Flood therapy is an extreme form of this. An example of flood therapy is taking someone who has acrophobia (a fear of heights) to the observation deck of a skyscraper. This form of treatment is effective for some people but a lot of people find it overwhelming, and it can make their phobias worse. A more effective approach has three steps that revolve around a gentler form of exposure.

Step 1: Gradual Exposure

This is when we expose ourselves to a mild situation that prompts anxiety, like a 2 or 3 out of 10 threat. A threat can refer to a threat to life or a threat to our ego. We're going to feel uncomfortable but if we sit with the discomfort, we'll see that we are safe. We may only need to experience this discomfort for a short while before our autonomic nervous system recognizes that we are not in any danger and our survival mode is reset.

Once we've become used to that level of threat, we can graduate to a 3 or 4 out of 10 threat and repeat the process. If this is done in a structured way, we should be able to go all the way up to a wrongly perceived 10 out of 10 threat. If we have too much difficulty sitting with the discomfort, the second step can be initiated.

Step 2: Self-regulation

This involves calming ourselves so the discomfort is minimized. There are different types of breathing exercises that work well. The one I use most often is box breathing, which is described in Chapter 1 (see box, page 37). If you're in the right environment, you could also try something called progressive muscle relaxation. There are two versions, which both involve going on a mental tour of your body and relaxing muscle groups. One of them involves relaxing the muscles you're focusing on; the other version involves tensing muscles for a couple of seconds first before relaxing them.

Box breathing and progressive muscle relaxation both work by inducing a state of relaxation. It's impossible for us to be anxious and relaxed at the same time, so if we are feeling anxious, inducing a state of relaxation through breathing will push the anxious state out. If the feelings are overwhelming, you can move onto the next step.

Step 3: Cognitive Restructuring

This involves educating our brain about why our body is responding in the way it is. It's engaging the prefrontal cortex so we can think more rationally. Practically speaking, it means talking to ourselves in a soothing way.

- We can remind ourselves of the three pillars of anxiety and remove one of them.
- We can remind ourselves that anxiety is just our survival mode activating unnecessarily.
- We can remind ourselves that our body is reacting as if we're in a life-threatening situation when we're not – just because we feel frightened, it doesn't mean that we are in danger.
- We can remember that the anxiety is the equivalent of an overprotective friend or an overprotective dog.

Taking on board any of these things should aid the process of self-regulation, which in turn aids the process of gradual exposure.

Key Takeaways

- The biggest obstacles to resilience are our emotions, and the main emotion that prevents resilience is anxiety.
- The more we know about anxiety, the more we can try to lessen its hold over us.
- We can reduce or even eliminate anxiety immediately through a variety of techniques.
- Once we've removed or reduced anxiety, we can take steps to improve our situation that we may not have taken before the anxiety showed up.

CHAPTER EIGHT

Memory Reconsolidation

Often the biggest obstacle to resolving anxiety is the anxiety itself. Someone who is extremely anxious is too anxious to do anything different because they're adopting a 'better the devil you know' stance. In this event, another process can be used, one that targets the memories that serve as scaffolding to the anxiety. This neurophysiological process – called memory reconsolidation – can overwrite neural pathways so that we can experience reality in a less maladaptive and more resilient way. This process will also give you a better understanding of why it's so hard to change consciously. Memory reconsolidation is also the best way to resolve trauma, reduce anxiety, improve resilience and make lasting change that's effortless to maintain. Every effective form of trauma treatment involves a memory reconsolidation component.

Making a Change

If we want to make a change and we're unable to, it implies a trauma response is active. Memory reconsolidation is very effective at resolving that trauma response so that we're able to make the change we want to make.

We can consider change, or going from A to B, as either an uphill struggle or a downhill journey. An example of an uphill struggle is the Six Stages of Change model. The stages are:

1. pre-contemplation (not yet knowing there's a need for change)
2. contemplation (recognizing the need for change)
3. determination (commitment to making the change)
4. action
5. relapse
6. maintenance

A NOTE ON TRAUMA

When I refer to 'trauma' in this chapter, it's in terms of a general trauma response, which includes little 't' trauma – small events that still have lasting impact. If you are experiencing significant trauma, I would recommend finding a suitable therapist to help you through the process, as there is a risk of re-traumatization.

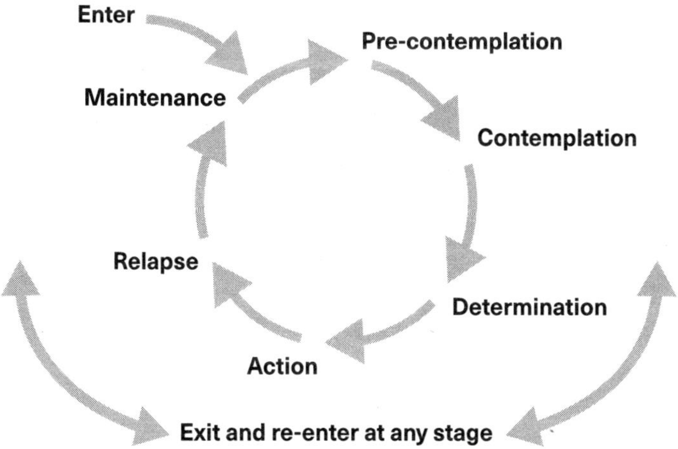

Figure 3: The stages of change

It's an uphill struggle because we must install a new behaviour. This behaviour is different to what we're currently doing, so we need to make a conscious effort until it becomes a habit. It involves skills, effort, practice and determination. Relapse is an important part of this model because sometimes, no matter how much we practise or how determined we are, we will fall back into the old routine because that's easiest or most familiar. With more effort, we can recover from relapses and the change can be maintained. With this model of change, we need to create a new neural pathway and practise it so the pathway is strengthened.

Unlike the uphill struggle, where new behaviours need to be installed, the downhill journey removes an obstacle to already installed behaviours. It presupposes that the change we're trying to make is something we've done in the past, but we're now stopping ourselves from doing it because we think something bad will happen.

The downhill journey can be represented by a downhill slalom skier. They are unable to proceed until the barrier preventing them from moving is removed. This barrier is a fundamental aspect of the trauma response. Your subconscious thinks if you proceed, you will be harmed. Your view of resilience is sometimes governed by your autonomic nervous system so it's outside of conscious control. You're naturally resilient only when you feel your safety isn't compromised. This makes it clear that trauma is a big factor in how resilient you feel.

Rewriting Neural Pathways

A very efficient method of resolving trauma or making any change is using the process of memory reconsolidation. It's the best way to evoke lasting change that's easy to maintain. This process overwrites the original neural pathway, which removes the opportunity for relapse, even for the most stressful of experiences. Your resilience will be unlocked and unobstructed.

A useful analogy is to think of us recording experiences and responses on one side of an audio cassette. Other types of trauma treatment will help us to record experiences on the other side of the cassette, and encourage us to practise just listening to that preferred side. However, in times of stress, we may automatically listen to the original side and respond in the way we don't want to. By contrast, memory reconsolidation records over the original recording, so relapsing is impossible. To respond in the way we used to, we would have to learn the response again.

Consolidation is the process of converting something that's held in short-term memory to long-term memory. Reconsolidation is updating the memory. Once something has been committed to long-term memory, we can usually update it easily. For example, you could erroneously learn that the capital of Bulgaria was a city called Ruse and hold that in your memory for years. If you then learnt the real capital is a city called Sofia, your memory can be easily updated.

Some things in our long-term memory can't be updated as easily because they're emotional memories, and those are encoded in a different way because they're more important. If, for example, we had experienced a traumatic event and developed a bee phobia as a result, it would be difficult to update that learning because our brain wants to hold on to the original idea that bees are dangerous to reduce the chances of being harmed by them again. That neural pathway is locked and inaccessible and is governed by the autonomic nervous system. We learnt that bees are dangerous and so we believe we're going to get stung every time we encounter one. We've since learnt otherwise, but the original pathway is still there.

We could try to reinforce the newer idea that bees aren't dangerous, but at best, we would create a neural pathway that competes with the original one. We might have confidence that we'd act appropriately until we're in the presence of a bee, when the original neural pathway will activate and the phobic response will be triggered, even if we tell ourselves that we shouldn't be scared.

Successful reconsolidation overwrites the original neural pathway so there's no chance of reactivation or relapse.

Prediction Errors

Memory reconsolidation works by targeting and activating the specific neural pathway, challenging the core prediction that is associated with it and then mismatching that prediction with a prediction error or mismatch experience. A prediction error or mismatch experience is an experience that directly contradicts the information already held. Mismatching the prediction once renders the pathway rewritable; we then have a window of four to five hours to rewrite the pathway. Rewriting is achieved by mismatching the prediction repeatedly up to three more times.

We can use the analogy of a three-drawer filing cabinet to show how this process works. The top drawer is where short-term memories are held. The middle drawer is reserved for non-emotional memories in our long-term memory, and the bottom drawer stores emotional memories in our long-term memory.

When you learnt the capital of Bulgaria, you transferred that information from the top drawer to the middle drawer.

You have free access to both drawers. If you ever need to update the information, you can open the middle drawer, find the relevant file and update your records.

When you learnt that bees were dangerous, you put that information into the bottom drawer. Unlike the other two drawers, this drawer is locked. It can only be opened by a specific process, which is identifying the relevant prediction and experiencing a prediction error or mismatch experience. This is how the process works:

1. Recall a time when you encountered a bee and were not harmed, while simultaneously reminding yourself of the prediction that you will be: 'Bees are dangerous – I will get stung every time I'm near one.' The bottom drawer is open, but the information is still inside.
2. The bottom drawer stays open for four to five hours – the rewrite window. Over this period, repeatedly bring to mind (at least three or four times) the memory or imagined experience of being unharmed by a bee. Two conflicting bits of information can't occupy the same space. Your brain labels one of them as true/more likely and the other as false/less likely. This process helps your brain label the two bits of information correctly. The false/less likely data (bees are dangerous) will be dropped and replaced with the updated information (bees are safe).
3. If you don't mismatch the experience during the rewrite window, the drawer will close and be locked again. It will only reopen if you restart the process – activating the pathway by identifying the prediction and mismatching it.

THE MEMORY RECONSOLIDATION EQUATION

There's an equation that demonstrates the components of memory reconsolidation:

activation + mismatch + repeat = rewrite[6]

Activation refers to us experiencing the fear response, where the autonomic nervous system is triggered. Mismatch involves us reminding ourselves of the prediction that underpins this response and experiencing something that directly contradicts the prediction. Repeating this process will overwrite the neural pathway, because when it comes to safety, the brain needs convincing in a more structured way.

If this technique doesn't work, it's likely you haven't identified the prediction so have edited the wrong neural pathway. If you have the right prediction but it still hasn't worked, it's likely the prediction error or mismatch experience hasn't landed as well as it could have. The prediction error needs to be significant. A bad prediction error is one you can explain away or provide exceptions for. A good prediction error is one you cannot ignore.

There are many ways that memory reconsolidation is achieved. A quick and easy way is to use an imaginary scene. This scene can be rooted in memory. Recall a memory where the unwanted response is prompted but after you experience the negative or unwanted sensations in the memory, you can reimagine the scene as if it went in your favour.

The Invisible Twin

A lot of professionals have contributed to the field of memory reconsolidation, including someone I've learnt from directly, psychotherapist Alun Parry. Alun conceived the idea of the invisible twin.

The idea of the invisible twin merges ideas of Polyvagal Theory, which describes the autonomic nervous system activity that keeps us safe. To summarize, we can say we have an invisible twin who steps in when it thinks we're doing or might do something harmful. The invisible twin thinks it's a better idea to do something different to the thing we want. It has a prediction and it's this prediction that is preventing us from doing something different.

I said in Chapter 6 (see page 105) that change is usually easy. It's only ever not easy when the invisible twin gets involved and stops us because they think there's danger. The invisible twin is invisible because we don't know the specific thing the twin fears and why. This information is vital for the process of change to work. We need to make the invisible twin visible, in order to find out why they think it's so important that we keep hold of this thing. We can then educate the twin and encourage it to stand down.

Psychologist and author Bruce Ecker has identified two stances a therapy client can take: an anti-symptom position and a pro-symptom position. The anti-symptom position is characterized by the client attending therapy with a problem they want to resolve. They don't like the problem. They're against it and want it gone. The invisible twin is a good way of personifying the pro-symptom position. The client with a pro-symptom position holds the viewpoint that it makes sense to carry on holding on to a behaviour or belief. The invisible twin thinks it's doing this for a good reason and it's fighting to maintain this symptom. It knows it's a problem but it thinks this problem is a solution to an even bigger problem.[7]

The Single Sentence Technique

The invisible twin's motivation can be made explicit by generating a sentence with a particular structure. The single sentence technique was initially devised by psychologist Niall Geoghegan and developed by Alun Parry.

The structure of the sentence is as follows:
'If I get [the good thing] or if I allow myself this [good thing],
then [the worst thing] will happen
so I do [the problem] instead even though I want [the good thing]
because ANYTHING is better than [the worst thing] (including [the problem]).'

Here's an example of a completed sentence:
'If I allow myself to be resilient,
I won't have any friends

so I become subservient even though I want to be resilient
because anything is better than not having friends
(including being subservient).'

And here is another:
'If I allowed myself to be more resilient at work,
I will take on too much work and get burnt out
so I don't take on things I want to do even though I want to be more resilient
because anything is better than being burnt out
(including turning down work I enjoy).'

From a certain point of view, it might seem a good idea to create a small amount of pain to avoid a large amount of pain. But in most situations that large amount of pain doesn't exist. This behaviour may have been useful in a specific scenario, but we apply to it to other situations in a blanket way.

The first two lines of the sentence are a prediction. We need to find out what the specific prediction is and use memory reconsolidation to mismatch that specific prediction to bring about a prediction error. Generally, the prediction is that getting the good thing will bring about the bad thing. Mismatching means recalling evidence that disproves this. We need a prediction error or a mismatch that will overturn the invisible twin's beliefs/motivation.

In the case of the second example above, the prediction is 'If I allowed myself to be more resilient at work, I will take on too much work and get burnt out'. Can you remember a time when you were resilient and *didn't* take on too much work? That is an experience that mismatches the prediction.

You may not even have to intentionally imagine or remember mismatches. If you remind yourself of the sentence often, the content of the sentence alone might enable you to see that it doesn't make absolute sense – especially if the bad thing that you are doing every time is worse than the worst thing (which may not even happen anyway). Everyday experience might spontaneously provide mismatches, depending on what the content of the single sentence is.

A Change of Perspective

You can try the single sentence technique for any change you want to make but feel unable to. If you can't make a change, that's because the invisible twin is stepping in and saying 'STOP!' because it thinks the cost of making that change is too high. The invisible twin believes this narrative is the best one because of its protective function. From a certain perspective that may be true, but it's demonstratively not true if you consider it from other perspectives.

In Chapter 3, we looked at how we sometimes hold on to what we think is the 'best' narrative (see page 62). We think some narratives are better than others because they're more realistic, more sensible or logical or more useful – which are the categories of best. We may think this because we're looking at the event from a very specific perspective, rather than entertaining other perspectives. If we changed our perspective, we would see a better narrative instantly, but sometimes we find the idea of changing our perspective counterintuitive, irrational or dangerous.

Memory reconsolidation is useful when the autonomic nervous system or invisible twin seems incapable of letting go of that 'not-best' perspective because it thinks your safety is compromised if you let go of it. It believes the cost of letting go is too high. Thinking about categories of best won't be enough in this scenario; we need to use memory reconsolidation to update memories by highlighting a prediction and then providing prediction errors at least three or four times. The first contradiction will open the neural pathway and prepare it to change. The subsequent contradictions will change it. The neural pathway will close and the new behavioural response will be automatic.

Key Takeaways

- There are two types of change: installing a new habit (uphill struggle) or removing obstacles to an old habit (downhill journey).
- Long-term emotional memories can only be updated through a process of memory reconsolidation.
- You can use your imagination to prompt reconsolidation by amending a memory and imagining it going in your favour.
- Our autonomic nervous system can be referred to as an invisible twin that resists change because it thinks this keeps us safe.
- The single sentence technique highlights the logic the invisible twin is using and makes it clear that the problem is a solution to a bigger problem.
- You may be stopping yourself from demonstrating resilience because you think the outcome will be negative, but continued lack of resilience is more negative.

CHAPTER NINE

Reparenting

The idea of the inner child was first discussed during the infancy of the psychoanalytic approach. It suggests that any issues we experience as adults stem from events that took place when we were children. In this chapter, we will travel back in time and reparent ourselves, so that we are able to respond to events in the now with more resilience. This may be of particular interest to anyone who considers themselves a perfectionist or control freak. It is possible to change our wiring, so that the idea of what is 'perfect' becomes less self-defeating.

The Inner Child

The concept of the inner child was introduced by the pioneering psychoanalyst Carl Jung in the 1910s. It saw a resurgence in the 1990s when a book written by John Bradshaw was published, and has become increasingly popular over the last decade or so.

The idea suggests that if the child is wounded, the adult will still experience the effects of that wound. To heal the adult, we have to heal the child. This child-centric way of healing trauma involves metaphorically travelling back in time and working with the child how they were back then, rather than working with the adult as they are now. What was going on for the child? What did that child need but didn't get? Once we have these answers, we can go back and reparent ourselves. We can reclaim, honour, champion and celebrate the child, which will have a bolstering effect on the adult.[8]

We can talk about self-compassion in either a child-focused or an adult-focused way. Just acknowledging that we have an inner child can have a significant positive impact and be rewardingly validating. Remember a time when our child had all the resilience it wanted. Try to think back to an event where this resilience started to erode or maybe a more significant event when it seemed to vanish. In some ways, your child might be metaphorically stuck in that time. That initial response could now be an automatically recurring response that you find extremely challenging to break free from.

We can imagine being kind to the child because that's something the child didn't perceive back then – we can give understanding, compassion, guidance. It may feel like the child is stuck in the past but it's not too late to do something about it. While less than ideal parenting increases the chances of resilience issues developing, they can still occur even if the child had 'sufficient' parenting. Our parents weren't with us all the time to know each challenging event we encountered. If they were with us during those events, they're not telepathic so they wouldn't know precisely how each event affected us. Even if they did, they (probably) were not child psychologists so could not respond to us in the best way, allowing us to adopt the best attitudes so that we could navigate future events more effectively.

There will always be an opportunity for us to reparent our inner child. We are the best person to reparent ourselves, in fact, because we were always present. Who knows the impact of our experiences better than us? We can re-evaluate critical moments from our past and finally integrate things that we may have consciously or subconsciously thought were missing, so that our natural resilience becomes emboldened instead of continuing to feel eroded.

Reparenting can be a constant process. We may not know that something is missing until we encounter an event that highlights this. Rather than criticizing ourselves for not noticing it previously, we can be thankful that we eventually caught and addressed it.

Attachment Issues

There are four main attachment styles: secure, anxious-preoccupied, dismissive-avoidant, and fearful-avoidant or disorganized. It is believed that each style is a response to how our caregivers responded to us when we were young.

If our caregivers responded to us appropriately and were not absent a lot of the time, we would develop a secure attachment style. This means we would find it easier to trust ourselves and others and have a positive view of ourselves and others. Resilience is strongly associated with the secure attachment style. Lower resilience is attached to all three of the other attachment styles.

The Ideal Parent Figure Protocol

I've often heard attachment styles referred to as if they're set in stone, but the work of Daniel Brown, a psychologist specializing in attachment, has proven otherwise.[9] Brown devised a technique called the ideal parent figure protocol that helps resolve attachment issues. He identifies five different areas that, if neglected, could lead to attachment issues:

- Safety and protection
- Attunement – being fully seen and known
- Reassurance and soothing
- Expressions of delight
- Unconditional support and encouragement

THE FOUR ATTACHMENT STYLES

- **Secure** – confident, trusting, resilient, high self-esteem, high resilience
- **Anxious-preoccupied** – anxious, insecure, clingy, fears rejection, low resilience
- **Dismissive-avoidant** – emotionally distant, over-independent, distrustful, low resilience
- **Fearful-avoidant or disorganized** – poor boundaries, extreme responses, low self-esteem, low resilience

The ideal parent figure protocol technique involves going back to key moments where you felt there were lapses in any of these areas and then reimagining those events as if we had different parents who responded to us in the precise way that we needed. For example, if we were to target a memory of a time when we felt unsafe – when we went to our parents and they responded to us in a way that we interpreted as dismissive – we can imagine different, ideal parents responding to us in a way that made it clear that we were safe and they would protect us if we were in danger.

Daniel Brown suggests imagining five different scenarios that match the five areas identified opposite. If the newly imagined scenes are imagined effectively, our attachment template should be updated. We would behave as if the ideal response had been given at the time. This process has been associated with memory reconsolidation because often reconsolidation occurs when you imagine past events going in a more favourable way.

This is a very simple and impactful process, but some people find it challenging for a few reasons. They find it difficult to imagine key events that involved their parents with anyone else. Some people have said that they find it somewhat disrespectful 'replacing' their parents in this way if they are able to. To be clear, the message is not necessarily that our parents did anything wrong when they were trying their best. They may have responded ideally in other areas that we're not thinking about. Due to negativity bias (see box, page 51), we're more likely to remember the times when things went wrong, not the times they went right.

If we have a problem replacing our parents with different parents, we could just imagine our parents responding to us in a different way that gave us what we needed at the time. Or we could just imagine going back ourselves and giving ourselves what we felt we needed.

'It's Okay'

I think it's a fair assumption that most children want to do the right thing. They often put pressure on themselves, which is counterproductive, or they punish themselves when they think they're not doing the right thing.

Ensuring our inner child receives the message at some point that it was okay to make mistakes when we were children would promote self-acceptance, and by extension promote resilience. Rather than placing too much emphasis on ideal outcomes, we could reinforce the benefits of being mindful more often because that will naturally lead to better outcomes.

If someone once told you something wasn't okay, it's possible that they were either having a bad day, projecting their undesired negative traits onto you or displacing their anger with someone else onto you. It might have been a throwaway comment to them but unfortunately for you, you internalized the message and made significant changes because of it.

You could revisit significant moments from your past and give your younger self the relevant message that would have been the most helpful to better navigate that situation:

- 'It's okay to look like that.'
- 'It's okay to think that way.'
- 'It's okay to feel/express your emotions.'
- 'It's okay to cry/be scared/make mistakes.'
- 'It's okay to be you.' In fact, 'It's okay to … [insert personality-affirming phrase here].'

These statements may sound obvious to the conscious mind, but if we had any maladaptive responses when we were younger, they were probably in response to someone directly or indirectly communicating to us that it wasn't okay to do the thing we just did or to be ourselves. Unfortunately, these messages were internalized and we're still carrying them around as subconscious programs. The child didn't hear these positive statements at critical moments, and they would probably benefit from hearing them now.

Reimagining Negative Emotions

Remember the Baby Theory, which we explored in Chapter 4 (see page 76)? By deconditioning our negative emotional responses in a parentally guided way, we can instil an excellent reframing attitude.

Imagine losing your favourite toy when you were six and telling your parents about it. Imagine your parents (and society) knew about the Baby Theory. This means, your parents will validate your feelings and will comfort you and will make it easier to feel better, while also making it clear that the worst thing about the event isn't the fact you don't have your favourite toy anymore – the worst thing about the situation is the fact that you're making yourself feel bad to try to rectify the situation. Your parents fully understand your deep sense of loss while making it clear to you that you don't need that particular toy to be happy, and even if you still felt you needed that toy to be happy, feeling bad isn't going to make it materialize.

Imagine if your parents were able to move you from a bad place of mourning the loss of your toy to a good place of being appreciative of all the things you still had. They would make clear that your happiness didn't depend on owning the toy. This would ideally result in you feeling better. If you're feeling better, you're more likely to look for the toy in a more relaxed, clear-headed and resourceful way and that would vastly increase the chances of finding it.

The above scenario is an ideal example of parenting by parents who are aware of the Baby Theory. Of course, even if your parents had known about this theory and tried to convey it to you when you lost your toy, you probably wouldn't have listened to them. You'd only be interested in getting your toy back because of your connection to it and how distraught you were. You wouldn't have had the mental dexterity to separate yourself from the situation in a more mature way and see it from an objective viewpoint – you would have just wanted your toy!

But imagine if your parents had responded in the same way *every time* you went to them and made it clear you were feeling bad. Above all, they would have comforted you while sensitively conveying the idea that the worst thing about the situation is the *feeling* and that's the part that you have control over. This could be the start of the generally helpful education that our negative emotions are self-generated. If your parents had responded in this way consistently from when you were the age of six, do you think you would still be having negative emotions for similar reasons by the time you were ten?

For those of us whose parents didn't nurture us in this way, we need to start doing it ourselves. Every time we have a negative emotion, we can firstly validate our feelings and comfort ourselves in the best way we can but make something as clear as possible: this negative emotion has a specific purpose that is making the situation worse, because it's instigating a state of learned helplessness, which is going to hinder our efforts to resolve the situation. It's the ultimate expression of self-defeating behaviour.

A Sensible Rule of Happiness – The Ab Mindset

We have rules of happiness and these rules began when we were children. We might find it difficult to change because these rules are subconscious and entrenched but the process might be easier than you think if we explore the logic that underpins them.

I've heard people express dissent at the idea that there can be a rule of happiness, almost like happiness can't be reduced to a formula. I think there absolutely is a rule. If there wasn't, we would find ourselves being happy randomly. We're happy when certain conditions are met. If we know what these conditions are, we're more likely to exert more influence to create these conditions.

We can generally have a sensible, healthy rule of happiness or an unhelpful and unhealthy one, and these can be packaged into two mindsets: an 'Ab' mindset and a 'z' mindset. The sensible mindset is the Ab mindset. That is, 'I have A, A is enough but I want b because b would be a pleasant addition.' So, you're happy anyway but you want something else that would lead to *more* happiness.

The unhelpful mindset, the z mindset is, 'I need z to be happy'. That means you're not happy because you're basing your happiness on something that you don't have. If someone is feeling negative or unhappy, they're clearly holding onto the rule, 'I need z to be happy', and they believe they don't have z. This means they're going to be unhappy until they get z or realize they don't need z to be happy.

We didn't start off with a z mindset. We started off thinking an equivalent of 'I have A, but A is not enough so I need b to be happy'. But, when we got b, we were happy for a while until we got bored of it or something better came along. We then subconsciously adopted the belief, 'I have A and b but that's not enough, so I need c to be happy'. When we got c, we were happy for a while until …

This unhealthy way of thinking continues all the way until we get to z and think, 'I have A–y but that's not enough, so I need z to be happy'. If we get z, we're happy for a while, then the z gets incorporated into the A–y. That makes space for another z and this means the odds of being genuinely and consistently happy are reduced, because there's always going to be something else that we want.

If this journey from b to z happened when we were older and more observant, we may have realized this thinking pattern was unhealthy when we got to e or f. Unfortunately, it happened when we were too young to have this awareness and so this insidious rule of happiness became ingrained to the point where a lot of people can't imagine things being any other way. That means some of us may always wholeheartedly believe that we do in fact need z to be happy.

Why Is the z Mindset Unhealthy?

The z mindset or rule is unhealthy and unhelpful for a few reasons including:

It Produces Self-defeating or Self-destructive Behaviour.
In our attempt to get z, we …

- ignore that we already have A–y
- devalue A–y
- in worst-case scenarios, can even destroy A–y

It Decreases the Chance of You Getting What You Want.
The neurophysiological effects of a desire are different to the effects of a need – the brain and the body work differently in those scenarios. If you merely *want* something, you're more likely to act in a way that increases the chances of securing the thing. You'll be more resourceful, flexible and able to problem solve better. If you think you *need* something, you may be more likely to act in a way that decreases the chances

> **PRISONER 119104**
>
> Viktor Frankl (Prisoner 119104) was an Austrian psychologist who was imprisoned in a German concentration camp during the Second World War. Despite what was happening in the world and the extreme ways Viktor and his loved ones were personally affected, he was able to remain positive. He's often regarded as the father of 'positive psychology'.
>
> Viktor wrote about some of his experiences in a book called *Man's Search for Meaning*.[10] He argues that your external circumstances are always secondary to your attitude. Your attitude can be tempered by a general way of thinking. He writes that if you know what the 'why' of the situation is, the body will work out the 'how'. He and other prisoners attested to this by withstanding the cruellest of treatment and conditions while remaining resilient, because they had at least one thing to be resilient for. If the reason is good enough, you will have access to an approriate amount of resilience, even in the harshest of conditions.

of securing that thing, due to the pressure you may be putting on yourself or others and the stress you feel, along with other unhelpful physiological effects.

It Makes You Less Able to Solve Problems.

With the z mindset, you'll see more problems and you won't be able to solve those problems as easily. With the Ab mindset, you'll see fewer problems and you'll deal with those problems more easily.

Happiness Is Based on Desires, Not Needs.

Comfort relates to needs. If our needs are met, we're comfortable. If our desires are met, we're happy. Thinking you *need* something to be *happy* doesn't make sense. After making the way the Ab mindset works explicit, that even if it might make you happier you don't *need* b to be happy, it might be easier to detect this illusion of need when it comes up and it most certainly will come up very frequently.

Key Takeaways

- Reparenting is an effective technique that can help us develop more resilience by reimagining our childhood.
- Self-acceptance promotes resilience. We can revisit our past and remind ourselves, 'It's okay'.
- There are invisible rules of happiness that we can appreciate to increase the chances of being happier more of the time.
- We can be resilient even in the harshest circumstances.

CHAPTER TEN

Where Do We Go From Here?

This book has outlined and detailed many ways to improve resilience. This chapter will summarize these and suggest ways of maximizing the benefits of what you've read and applying it. It will also provide examples of some different road maps you can use to help restore resilience. Creating road maps can be a useful way of systematically integrating this information. You could repeat different versions that reinforce the idea of 'I am resilient!' or 'I can be resilient!' until you believe it. Alternatively, you can challenge any thoughts that contradict the idea that you're resilient.

Rethinking Resilience

It all starts with a thought. A thought can come in any shape: it can be a sound, a symbol, a word or any other type of data. We can identify our thoughts. Some of them have subconscious origins and remain subconscious; others are more immediately identifiable. We have the tools to identify our subconscious thoughts. Our thoughts only have the power that we give to them. If we have a negative thought, we can either accept it or challenge it. We often have negative thoughts about ourselves, rather than being self-compassionate.

Self-compassion can be a lifelong endeavour. We want the best for ourselves but we can either criticize ourselves to achieve it, or encourage ourselves to achieve it. We will certainly achieve it more easily if we encourage ourselves rather than criticize, because of the often-negative emotional response we have to criticism.

We can mentally rehearse situations we find challenging and practise them. The more we mentally rehearse, the more likely it is that we'll react in the way that we want when the situation arises. Once we're no longer experiencing the challenging situation, we can bounce back from it if we didn't handle it as well as we would have liked to. (Chapter 1)

We can look at the situation in a different way by trying one of the different types of reframing. You can positively reframe and acknowledge that positive things can follow on from negative situations. You can nominate another person and see the situation from their perspective. How is that person looking at the situation so that resilience is maintained? You can acknowledge you can entertain multiple perspectives, but are only supposed to entertain the *best* of them. Starting points matter. Are you assuming a victim stance, or a more helpful survivor stance or warrior stance? (Chapter 3)

Are you presupposing a state of resilience or are you presupposing that you don't have resilience? If you see resilience as something that's innate, it will be a lot easier to experience it more consistently. If you're forgetting that at one time resilience was a given and now believe it's a skill that needs to be learnt, what's preventing you from learning it more easily? (Chapter 2)

We are all motivated by the idea of better but often the idea of better is the illusion of better because other choices have not been made apparent. Is it a simple case of gain or pain? Or is it a slightly more complicated choice of short-term gain/long-term pain versus short-term pain and long-term gain?

Are you focusing on what you want or what you don't want? You can still secure desired outcomes by focusing on what you don't want, but you may find it a lot easier to get there by focusing on what you do want. (Chapter 1)

Look After Yourself

Our emotional state is tied to our physical state and sleep is a big factor for our physical state. You can increase the chances of getting a better night's sleep by exposing yourself to daylight in the morning, not eating too close to bedtime, restricting your screen time before bedtime and focusing on

A NOTE ABOUT THE ROAD MAPS

The road maps in this chapter are examples of attitudes you can adopt, or questions you can ask, to increase your resilience. Feel free to use these or create your own personal ones based on experiences or ideas and tweak them as you go.

relaxing rather than trying to fall asleep. If you find yourself unable to fall asleep because of overthinking, allocate yourself a certain amount of time to think about a problem or resolve 'what ifs' by answering the implicit question. You can imagine being in the same position you're in now but as if that past event had unfolded how you wanted it to. (Chapter 1)

The Role of Thoughts, Feelings and Emotions

Our thoughts and narratives lead to feelings. We can reframe our thoughts to experience different feelings. Our emotional responses are logical, precise and purposeful. If you are experiencing a negative feeling, remind yourself of the Baby Theory. Our negative emotions are a remnant of a problem-solving mechanic we needed as babies but which is still running, even though we no longer need it. That means all negative emotions, including stress, are created in an entirely proactive process. We don't encounter stressful experiences – we encounter experiences and we subconsciously think feeling stress is the best way to deal with them.

A PRE-EMPTIVE ROAD MAP

This road map helps to consolidate a mindset that will allow you to navigate challenging situations in the future with more confidence. It focuses equally on withstanding challenges and on bouncing back from them. Following the ideas in this road map will likely take some of the pressure off and enable you to be more resourceful, which will increase the chances of things going your way. If things don't go your way, you'll be more reflective and encouraging, rather than critical.

Things you can do to prepare for upcoming events:

- Mental rehearsal.
- Remind yourself that it matters only as much as you say it does.
- Remind yourself that the moment will come and it will pass.
- Presuppose resilience – remember that you have resilience unless you're blocking it.
- If you think you are blocking resilience because of negative feelings, change those feelings by looking at the event in a different way.
- If you feel stuck, identify the prediction that's underpinning the obstacle, create a prediction error and repeat three or four times to rewrite the neural pathway.
- Remember that you are going to accept yourself, no matter what happens.

Every negative emotion is a reflection of an unmet wish. What's the wish at the core of your current negative emotion?

Our negative emotions are often the biggest obstacles to our levels of resilience. Learning how to manage our emotions better will remove this obstacle. (Chapter 4)

Our negative emotions are possible only because we're falling for four illusions at the same time – illusions of better, need, discomfort and control. Different analogies can be useful to identify these illusions and reprogram our brains to better understand our emotional responses. (Chapter 5)

Aim For a Growth Mindset

The quality of our thoughts stems from our mindset. Even if we have doubts about the Baby Theory, we can still manage our emotions better. We could just practise reframing the situation or change our mindset. Are we currently exhibiting a fixed mindset or a growth mindset? Are we making it easier or harder to achieve what we want? In terms of happiness, do we have an Ab or a z mindset? Are we creating a rule of happiness that means in the long-term happiness will remain elusive?

We were all born resilient. The brain works by inhibiting – we can do anything we want (laws of physics permitting) unless we tell ourselves that we can't or shouldn't. What happened was this: an event occurred, someone responded to us in a way that we found challenging so we changed our behaviour to protect ourselves and to avoid similar events in the future. In a lot of situations, that protection is causing us a lot more upset than the thing we're trying to protect ourselves from. (Chapter 6)

A SPONTANEOUS ROAD MAP

This road map focuses primarily on withstanding a challenging situation. The ideas and questions will nurture an accepting attitude towards yourself and the other person (if applicable) and will bolster resilience. It will also nurture a more flexible attitude and encourage you to be kind to yourself, no matter what else happens.

Things you can do during challenging events:

- Be mindful – remind yourself these moments will pass.
- Remind yourself that it's okay – be self-compassionate.
- Where someone else is involved, other person reframe – try to increase empathy towards the other person and realize that, like you, they're probably doing the best they can.
- Check your stance: are you entertaining a survivor stance, a warrior stance or a victim stance?
- Consider what you ***want*** to get out of the situation. Are you saying that you ***need*** it? Can you accept not getting it?
- Ask yourself if getting what you want is a case of short-term gain but long-term pain?
- Remind yourself that have more than enough resilience to navigate situations much more challenging than this one.
- Remember that simply being alive in this moment is infinitely more important than the outcome.

What About Trauma & Anxiety?

We should be able to change our behaviour easily. The only time we're unable to change our behaviour is when we feel we would be exposing ourselves to risk by doing so. This is a trauma response. Anxiety is often a consequence of trauma responses. We can de-escalate anxiety or remove it by learning more about it (Chapter 7). We can use the memory reconsolidation process if we're unable to de-escalate anxiety by other means. That involves targeting specific neural pathways and updating them so the trauma response is overwritten. Our habits are encoded within the cerebellum. We don't have to think about acting or thinking in a certain way; it's automatic. To disrupt these unhelpful automatic programs, we need to use the cortex in a conscious way and if we do, in time, new, more helpful thoughts will replace the unhelpful ones. (Chapter 8)

Nurturing Our Resilience

We were unquestionably resilient when we were children. If it was effortless then, it can be effortless again. As we grew older, we encountered events that inhibited this natural response. We can reparent our inner child so that we as adults can respond in a more healthy way. We can communicate with that child and give it what it needed at the time in order for it not to have to respond in a maladaptive or unhealthy way. If the child had understood that it was okay, we would have responded differently then and would behave differently now. It's never too late to communicate that it's okay.

A RETROSPECTIVE ROAD MAP

This road map focuses primarily on bouncing back from challenging events and shortening the turnaround time so that you recover quicker. Reflecting on events is an important process because a large percentage of our thoughts is dedicated to the past. There's only our past and our memories of it, the ever-escaping now and our view of a potential future. Having a structured reflective process will increase the chances of bouncing back from challenging events healthily and quickly.

Things you can do to move forward after a challenging event:

- Remind yourself that event had to happen for you to be here in this now.
- Ask yourself if there is anything you can do differently to increase the odds of a favourable outcome in the future.
- Remember that your existence implies resilience.
- Consider what you would say to the past version of you to feel better.
- Identify if there is an unmet wish. Is there anything you can do to meet it? Can you ask someone for assistance? Or can you accept it can't be met?
- Ask if you can accept yourself. If not, what can't you accept?
- Remember self-acceptance is universal and unconditional.
- If you're still feeling negatively about the event, how quickly can you expose any of the four illusions (of better, need, discomfort and control) that are underpinning your negative emotional response?
- Determine if you are exhibiting an Ab mindset or a z mindset about the past event.

We have more resilience than we need, but it needs to be consciously accessed sometimes. If we identify a reason to be resilient, it will naturally happen again.

We can acknowledge that our emotions are there to help, not hinder. Exploring negative emotions may help you see that life could be very different, very easily. If we're preventing ourselves from being a more authentic version of ourselves, that might be evidence of a recurring maladaptive response. If we better understood the response, we may find the positive intent is being overshadowed by the negative impact – it was done for a good reason but may not be securing ideal responses. Being kinder to ourselves will help us access better emotions. Those better emotions will help us navigate challenging situations more easily. (Chapter 9)

We have a tremendous capacity to withstand challenging events naturally. Even if we didn't, we have a tremendous capacity to bounce back from them and return to a more preferable state. If there's an issue with either of these two innate abilities, there are many ways we can explore obstacles and resolve them. Challenging issues are opportunities to learn, develop and thrive. It may then be a lot easier to nurture a mindset with peace, kindness and resilience at its core.

Endnotes

1 *Oxford English Dictionary* (7th edition, 2012). Oxford. OUP.

2 Maltz, M. (1960). *Psycho-Cybernetics.* New Jersey. Prentice Hall.

3 'Serenity Prayer'. In: Niebuhr, R. (ed.) (1951). *The Meaning of the Message.* New York: Simon and Schuster.

4 Dweck, Dr C. S. (2017). *Mindset – Changing the way you think to fulfil your potential.* London. Robinson.

5 *Dogs Behaving (Very) Badly*, Season 4, Episode 13 (22 March 2022). Channel 5.

6 Parry, A. (2022). *How to Remove Trauma Response – A Memory Reconsolidation Guidebook for Therapists and Coaches.* Fresh Therapists.

7 Quoted in: ibid.

8 Bradshaw, J. (1990). *Home Coming – Reclaiming and championing your inner child.* London. Piatkus.

9 Brown, D. P. & Elliot, D. S. (2016). *Attachment Disturbances in Adults: Treatment for Comprehensive Repair.* New York. WW Norton & Co.

10 Frankl, V. (1946). *Man's Search for Meaning.* London. Rider.

About the Author

Byron Athene is a counselling psychotherapist, clinical supervisor, certified mindset coach and hypnotherapist in private practice. He's also a trainer and an author.

He's been interested in psychology and philosophy for more than 30 years and since qualifying as a therapist and life coach in 2020, he has gained many qualifications that have helped him increase his effectiveness. He has an unshakeable belief in the unlimited capacity for people's ability to heal and improve.

He specializes in emotions and can guide his clients to a mindset that allows them to have mastery over their emotions and maximize their potential as a direct result. He has developed his own therapeutic approach, which is a revolutionary modality that seamlessly integrates ancient philosophy with cutting-edge psychology and neuroscience.

He's also a serial podcast guest, discussing a range of topics related to psychoeducation and self-improvement.

Index

Ab mindset 142–6, 152, 155
acceptance 19, 21, 44, 47, 139, 146, 153, 155
ACE Framework, the 50–5, 66
agency 53, 63, 64
agreement principle 33
amygdala 27
analogies, for deconditioning 91–3, 98, 152
anger 64, 65, 72, 75, 76, 139
anti-symptom position 127, 128
anxiety 11, 30, 31, 46, 72, 111–19, 154
  three pillars 112, 113, 117
attachment styles 136
autonomic nervous system 107, 116, 122, 123, 126, 127, 131, 132
avoidance 30, 31, 71, 76, 102, 103, 113

Baby Theory (negative emotions) 76–83, 86, 91–8, 140, 141, 150, 152
best perspective reframing 61–70
better, illusion of 29–32, 42, 87, 89, 91, 98, 130, 149, 152, 155
biases, *see* negative confirmation bias, neutral bias, positive confirmation bias, primary bias
bouncing back, from challenges 7, 12, 63, 65, 68–71, 100, 148, 151, 155, 156
box breathing 37, 40, 116
Bradshaw, John 134
brain, *see* amygdala, cerebellum, neocortex, neuroscience, prefrontal cortex, thalamus
Brown, Daniel 136, 137

cerebellum 27, 154
challenge-based response, *see* eustress, stress
change, *see* growth mindset, Six Stages of Change model
circadian rhythms 38–40
Cognitive Behaviour Therapy (CBT) 20, 46
cognitive restructuring 117
comfort 30, 31, 76, 77, 86, 87, 140–42, 146
compliance principle 33, 34
conditioned responses 81, 82, 85, 91, 98
conscious mind, the 14, 19, 26, 29, 33, 34, 40, 57, 64, 66–9, 79, 92, 102, 105, 106, 108, 119, 121, 122, 135, 139, 154
  see also, subconscious, the
control 25, 40, 45, 47, 49, 53–5, 74, 87, 88, 90, 91, 93, 98, 113, 122, 133, 141, 152, 155
  freak, *see* perfectionists
  illusion of 87, 88, 90, 91, 98, 152, 155
cortex 107, 154

deconditioning 91, 98
defusing techniques 36
demands 20, 21
discomfort 30, 31, 76–83, 116
  illusion of 87, 88, 90–2, 98, 152, 155
distress 22
Dweck, Dr Carol 100

Ecker, Bruce 127
Ellis, Albert 46
emotional responsibility, principles of 54, 55
emotions 43, 50, 51, 52, 69, 81, 83, 85–8, 99, 118, 123, 140, 141, 150
  stages of development 86–8, 96, 98
  see also, negative emotions
empowerment 54, 63, 67, 68
Epictetus, Stoic philosopher 53, 54
equilibrium 76, 77, 86, 87
eustress 22

fixed mindset 10, 100–04, 108, 110, 152
flood therapy 115
Frankl, Viktor
  Man's Search for Meaning 145
functional fixedness 59, 60
Function Theory (negative emotions) 74, 75, 78

Geoghegan, Niall 128
gradual exposure, to threat 116–18
grief 60
growth mindset 10, 99–110, 152

happiness, rule of 142, 146, 152
homeostasis, *see* equilibrium
hypnotherapy 11, 40

ideal parent figure protocol 136–9
illusions, *see* better, control, discomfort, need
Inevitability Theory (negative emotions) 74, 75
inhibitory nature of the brain 105, 106, 152
inner child 133–9, 154
invisible twin, the 127–32

Jung, Carl 134

kiki, Japanese for 'crisis' 61

lateral thinking 59
logic 72, 106–08, 110, 130, 132, 150
long-term gain 31, 149, 153

maladaptive response 108, 119, 139, 154
Maltz, Maxwell
 Psycho-Cybernetics 32
maximal direction 34
memory 23, 45, 119–32, 137, 138, 154, 156
mental rehearsal 25–9, 42
mindfulness 36–8, 40, 42, 138, 153
mindset, *see* Ab mindset, fixed mindset, growth mindset, z mindset
mirroring 46, 47
mismatching 124–6, 129–30
moral codes 72
motivation 22, 25, 29, 30, 47, 74, 75, 92, 107, 108, 128, 149

narratives 43, 49–55, 57, 62–70, 83, 99, 130, 150
need 76–83, 146, 150, 153
 illusion of 87–9, 91, 98, 146, 152, 155
negative confirmation bias 15, 51
negative emotions 9, 23, 33, 46, 47, 50, 51, 52, 55, 58, 61, 62, 63, 66, 70–83, 85, 88–98, 110, 140, 141, 148, 150, 151, 152, 156
negativity bias 51, 58, 78, 138
neocortex 27, 28
neurodivergence 80
neuroscience 27–9, 33, 34, 41, 64, 66, 105–07, 116, 119, 121–26, 131, 144, 154, 156
neutral bias 16

Niebuhr, Reinhold
 Serenity Prayer 44

Onoda, Hiroo 92, 93
other person reframing 59, 60, 153

parent figure 136–9
parenting 133–42, 146
Parry, Alun 127, 128
perception 13, 45–55, 72, 99, 101, 104, 111
perfectionists 133
perspective 37, 52, 53, 54, 57–8, 148, 149
 changing 130, 131, 151
 reframing 61–70
Polyvagal Theory, the 127
positive confirmation bias 17, 51
positive reframing 58, 59
positive thinking 32
prediction error 124–7, 129–32, 151
preferences 20, 21
prefrontal cortex 27, 28, 41, 117
pressure, *see* stress
primary bias 51, 58, 79
Prisoner 119104 145
progressive muscle relaxation 116
pro-symptom position 127, 128
protection paradox 99, 108–10

rational approach 32, 33
Rational Emotive Behaviour Therapy (REBT) 20, 46, 47, 55
reality, model of 45–55
reconsolidation, of memory 119–32, 137, 138, 154
recovering, *see* bouncing back, from challenges
reframing 57–71, 76, 83, 140, 148, 149, 150
 anxiety 111–18
reparenting 133–46, 154
reversed effect, law of 22, 23
road maps to restore resilience 147, 151, 153, 155
rotoscoping 48–50, 54, 55

self-acceptance 21, 139, 146, 155
self-compassion 19, 20, 42, 134, 148, 153, 156
self-esteem 8, 11, 20, 137
self-image 8, 19
self-regulation 116–18
self-worth 8, 105

sensory receptors 45, 49
Serenity Prayer 44, 97
short-term pain 31, 149, 153
Single Sentence Technique, the 128–30, 132
Six Stages of Change model, the 120–22, 127
skills, transferring 35
sleep 38–42, 149, 150
Solution-focused Brief Therapy approach 32–5
stances, survivor, victim or warrior 63, 64, 149, 153
Stoicism 44, 45, 47, 52, 53, 55
stories, *see* narratives
stress 22–5, 42, 123
  four pillars of 23–5, 42, 112
stuck states 47
stuttering 8, 10, 11
subconscious, the 14, 18–19, 26, 29, 30, 33, 40, 46, 51, 53, 57, 64, 66–9, 74, 79–82, 87, 90, 93, 96–8, 105, 106, 108, 114, 115, 122, 135, 140, 142, 143, 148, 150
  see also, conscious mind
symptoms 127, 128

thalamus 27, 28, 33, 41
thoughts, impact on experience 13–19, 24, 25, 27–9, 32–8, 40–2, 99, 145, 147–50
threat 72, 99, 111–13, 115–19
  threat-based response, *see* distress, stress
trauma 11, 32, 105, 108, 119, 120, 122, 134, 154
turnaround time 68–70, 155

unconscious, *see* subconscious

visualization, *see* mental rehearsal

withstanding challenges 4, 12, 63, 69, 70, 71, 145, 151, 153, 156
Wygal, Winnifred
  Serenity Prayer 44

z mindset 143–5, 152, 155

The *Find Your Path* Series

Find Your Path books shed light on a range of common mental-health struggles, from depression to imposter syndrome, and offer powerful techniques for navigating life's inevitable ups and downs.

Find Your Path through Anxiety: Mindful techniques to help you find ease (2025)

Find Your Path through Depression: Mindful techniques for dark times (2025)

Find Your Path through Imposter Syndrome: Powerful techniques to help you see your worth (2025)

Find Your Path to Resilience: Powerful techniques to build emotional strength (2025)

Find Your Path to Compassion: Powerful techniques to lead you to kindness (2025)